Teaching Children the Gospel

How to Raise Godly Children

~~~~~~~~~~~~~~~~~~~~~~~~~~~~~~~~~~~~

By Jack Wellman

Table of Contents

	Introduction	P. 6
Chapter One:	Developing Godly Children	P. 11
Chapter Two:	Teaching the Gospel to Children	P. 21
Chapter Three:	Become As Little Children	P. 30
Chapter Four:	What is The Age of Accountability?	P. 36
Chapter Five:	The Three Types of Parents	P. 45
Chapter Six:	How to Talk About Sex with Children	P. 50
Chapter Seven:	How to Discipline Children in Love	P. 58
Chapter Eight	Keeping Children in the Church	P. 65
Chapter Nine	Ways to Teach Children the Bible	P. 74
Chapter Ten	The Importance of Parents	P. 101

Teaching Children the Gospel, 3rd Volume. Copyright © 2015 by Jack Wellman
ISBN 1449996388   EAN-13 9781449996383

Introduction

For many years I have taught Sunday school and I refer to them as my children even though today I am a pastor, but really even my own children and grandchildren are not really mine. They are Gods. He has entrusted them to us but for a time. Children are a gift of God but someday they must go out into the world on their own. We only have them for a relatively short period of time. I have taught Sunday school to young children since around 1980 but I must admit that they have actually taught me more than I believe I have ever taught them.

Rather than asking children if they want to get saved, if they want to accept Jesus, or want Jesus to come into their heart in the hopes that they might be saved it is much better to ask open-ended questions, like "What do you think about Jesus?" or "Who is Jesus to you?" I never ask them if they want to be saved because they might do it for me or for the wrong reasons. I never, ever want to pressure children into being saved. I don't want to take the place of the Holy Spirit Who is the One Who reveals their need for a Savior. God knows when the best time is for them to believe in Jesus Christ, I don't.

I worked with Migrant Head Start and spoke Spanish for several years and when I worked with the parents and young children, I always tried to speak to both the parents and to the children in their language. Bad as my Spanish was, they sometimes got a good laugh when I butchered their beautiful language. Once I was speaking to a group of parents in Spanish and told them that I was embarrassed to speak in front of large groups. Instead of telling them I was embarrassed, I told them I was pregnant! The words pregnant and embarrassed are so close that I got them mixed up but they didn't care. I think they liked my honesty and me laughing at myself. But the children took it literally!

When I trained the teachers for the classrooms, I taught large groups at the same time. I always asked for their input in my training sessions and when you get a large group of teachers together, you've got years of wisdom and knowledge. I would learn from them and then incorporate their comments into my next training session. That is what I've tried to do teaching Sunday school and today as a pastor I am still a student. Children teach me many things. I openly and honestly admit that I make mistakes and by admitting my flaws they realize that it's okay to make mistakes and it's good to admit to them when you do. This is part of learning but I was learning too and I wanted them to know it!

That is what this book is about; a gleaning of ideas from educators, administrator, college professors, from the children themselves, but ultimately, from the Word of God, the Bible. I want to share this with parents, teachers, grandparents, and anyone else who comes into contact with children. Presenting the gospel to children is similar to presenting it to adults but with important differences. The Gospel is so easy to understand that even a young child can understand it but there are differences in the language that you use than you would with adults. Children are concrete thinkers and do not typically think in abstract ways. The way to present the gospel is in simple, concrete, and literal language. It's about believing in Jesus; trusting in and relying upon Him. It's not about letting Him come into their heart, having them repeat a sinner's pray, filling out a decision card, or accepting Him. It's all about belief, trust, and repentance. It shows what saving faith is, how they learn to believe in Christ, and what sin is and why we need to confess our sins. Let's follow the way of the Master and not preconceived ideas that are abstract.

Chapter One

Developing Godly Children

Scripture teaches that children develop in four areas and these areas are the same areas that Jesus developed in. Luke 2:52 records that Jesus grew in four distinct areas that children are designed to grow in.

1. In wisdom (mentally)

2. In favor with mankind (socially)

3. In favor with God (spiritually)

4. In stature (physically)

Development in children includes discipline because God disciplines adults and it is a prerequisite to growing in grace and knowledge. As the Bible teaches, God disciplines those that He loves, otherwise, we're simply illegitimate children (Prov. 3:11). Obedience in children flows naturally out of love, for without love you're only a drill sergeant as far as the children are concerned. Ephesians 4:6 tells us that we risk provoking them to anger, and an angry child will gravitate to disobedience, just as any adult would. True child abuse is leaving a child to themselves. Hate is not the opposite of love...apathy is. Of course, physical or sexual abuse is incomprehensible, not to mention punishable by law and you can wreck a child's life and increase the chances of them becoming an abuser as well but parental neglect and a child left with no discipline is like telling the child you don't really love them and that you don't care about them. By treating a child like that, you are setting them up to repeat the same thing in their families.

Even the non-Christian world understands that a lack of discipline and love leads to a child's feeling unworthy and disobedient. In a study by Harvard University, called Unraveling Juvenile Delinquency sociologists, Sheldon and Eleanor Glueck pinned down four critical areas that will prevent a child from becoming a delinquent and a future criminal.

1. The father's firm, fair, and consistent discipline.

2. The mother's supervision and companionship.

3. The parents' demonstrated affection for each other and for the children.

4. The family's cohesiveness: time spent together in activities where all can participate.

Harvard's sociologists didn't get this from the Bible, but it says exactly the same thing.

Provoking children comes in many forms:

1. Verbal, physical or sexual abuse

2. Neglect

3. Lack of discipline

4. Lack of limitations or structure and over protectionism

5. Favoritism

6. Discouragement

7. Overindulgence or under-indulgence

Parents are in the greatest position to model the love of God and Jesus Christ than anyone else on earth. If fathers and mothers are tyrants then that is the image they will have of God. Perhaps the five most important words that you can ever tell your children (or anyone for that matter) is, "I love you" and "I'm sorry". When they realize that parents admit mistakes and ask for forgiveness, then children can see that it's okay to make mistakes and admit them too. It also show that forgiveness is not just a child's standard, its everyone's standard and by admitting your mistakes to the children and are far from they see it as natural to make mistakes in life. When parental love is strong, this models and enhances the love of the child to parents. They might giggle or cover their eyes when daddy kisses mommy or mommy kisses daddy, but inwardly, this is very comforting to the child. It builds confidence in the family structure and exhibit's a safe feeling for the child. It gives the child a sense of security and steadfastness like nothing else can.

What' does this have to do with raising godly children in the hopes that they trust in Jesus Christ as their Lord and Savior? God loved us first even when we didn't deserve it. When a child is at their worst behavior is actually the time when the child needs your love the most. <u>When they are the most unlovable you have to be the most loving toward them.</u>

It is critical to remember that anything a parent can do, they can still not bring a child to salvation. Even though this is the greatest need that any young child has, this is still the work of the Holy Spirit alone (John 3:8). We can fertilize and water, but God always gives the increase. No child should ever feel pressured to get saved. Adults don't like to be pressured and neither do children. We never know when a child will be ready to trust in Christ. It's not the parent's job to know when the best time is or when the best time isn't. God knows. That's all we need to know.

As a father and grandfather, I am continually surprised at just how intelligent children really are. I will not sit in judgment and say, "well, you're too young" or "you're really not ready yet to be saved." Only God knows the heart and if they talk to the pastor or you and he or you feel that they are ready then it may be time. Never tell them that they're too young. Even in the event that they do not fully understand the gospel, they may be in early stages of understanding the gospel because someone has planted a seed and that seed must not over or under-watered. <u>It may be that a mature faith will ~~sprout~~ from this at a later time.</u> God alone knows.

Spiritual transformation is the same in a 90 year-old as it is in a 9 year-old. If there is a willingness to trust in Jesus (John 10:27), to love others (1 John 3:14), to confess their sins to God (1 John 1:9), to obey God (John 15:14) and repent and do what is right (John 17:6), then this may be a sign your child wants to be saved. You might notice that most of these evidences are from the apostle John. If a child wants to read about it, encourage them to do so. I recommend the gospel of John because he is known as the "disciple that Jesus loved" and his writings reflect the nature of the love of Jesus Christ and His divinity.

I am not saying that parents should not stress a need for salvation and Jesus as their Savior, but they must allow the child to come to this faith by themselves. I have heard of many who were saved as a young child only to live a life that showed no fruit of conversion. A later conversion is better than a pressured (and false) one. The evidences of their beliefs and confessions will make it clear if they understand it or not. We shouldn't give them a false sense of security in salvation if they are *not* saved but neither should we question their sincerity either. God alone knows the heart. Most children will sincerely know when they feel convicted by the Holy Spirit. Some may choose saving faith in Christ at an early age like my daughter who was saved and baptized at age seven.

Child-like faith expressions should not be taken as childish, immature or trivial. They should be considered seriously. External actions are *not* a way to confirm nor deny a child's being ready to trust in Christ, like, "just read this sinner's prayer" or "just let Jesus come into your heart." We already know that this is not based upon a belief or inner conversion, but more like jumping through hoops, like a trained dog. The only outward expressions of an inward conviction are baptism, but baptism comes *after* a person's salvation. An inward conviction of belief will reveal itself in language that the child uses, but an altar call alone may not be confirming enough above all other evidence. It is considerably rash to rush and have the child dunked immediately after an expression of salvation into baptism. It should be made clear that there is no salvation in getting baptized. It is only an outward expression of an inward conviction. And a rush to baptize a child may make them think that they are not saved until they are baptized, which for the thief on the cross, was not even possible.

Encourage obedience from the perspective of this being the right thing to do and not a life of obedience from the fear of punishment but prefer a tearful conversion and not a fearful one. Foxhole conversions are rarely sincere and lasting. Internal responses of obedience from scripture are more valuable than the fear of consequences of disobedience because there will be times when no one is watching (but God) and internal lotuses of control have more lasting value than parental peer pressure. Children will be saved by the power of the Word of God and no child (or adult) will be saved apart from the Cross of Christ (the Gospel) by the work of the Holy Spirit. Teaching children about the Fall of Mankind and their need of a Savior is a necessary part of this salvation. Their need to surrender and ask for forgiveness is before God and not parents. However, just verbalizing the Gospel is useless if a parent is not living up to it. Our children cannot hear us even if we shout out the Gospel message because what we are doing is drowning out anything we could ever say.

I do not recommend having a party if a child gets saved. If I asked my 3rd and 4th graders in Sunday school, "Who here is saved?" if one hand shoots up then the others will out of peer pressure. If I ask, "Who wants to be saved today?" they may do it to please me and not be a work of the Holy Spirit. A great balance should be implemented. On the one hand, we don't want children to profess Christ without understanding what they are really doing, but on the other hand we don't want to disbelieve a genuine calling to repentance and salvation. Clearly though, with no thought of repentance, there likely is no real call to salvation, for godly repentance is part of the calling of all those who will be or have been saved.

Caving into parental wishes or parental pressures may cause the child to feel like they need to be saved to please their parents. This can also cause a false call to conversion and salvation. This goes for the grandparents, aunts and uncles, foster parents, Sunday school teachers and for any other significant person in the child's life. It is understood that there is nothing more joyful to a parent, grandparent or Sunday school teacher than to have a child get saved, but it must be sincere and of a work of the Holy Spirit, or it is fruitless and can do more harm than good.

There is danger in oversimplifying the Gospel or using a canned process, filling out a decision card, abbreviating it, using a particular formula or repeating a sinner's prayer. This threatens the legitimacy of the Gospel and downplays the sacrificial atonement of Jesus' shed blood. Conversely, we don't want to make the Gospel so complicated that the child gives up in discouragement from its ambiguity. One thing must be clear. It is the Gospel's accuracy and using the Word of God for we already know that God's Word is powerful, effective, and never returns void or without effect (Isaiah 55:11). The Spirit of God makes the children of God and it is never the product of the human will.

Basic concepts such as the Fall, good and evil, consequences of all humans being sinners, the fact that Jesus is God and came as a human to die for humans as the perfect Lamb of God sacrifice, His atoning work of the cross, His death, resurrection and ascension into heaven and His Lordship are all elements that must be included in presenting the Gospel. The Word of God is truth and the Gospel must be wholly presented as such. The Holy Spirit is more than able to convert the soul (Prov 21:1). Humans never have been nor can ever be the agent of conversion and repentance. This alone is the Work of God and decidedly not the work of teachers or parents.

The way to present and teach the Gospel equally applies to adults too. It must be presented in its entirety. It is my purpose and my prayer that this may be helpful in bringing many into the kingdom of heaven, children included. But this will not happen without the redemptive power and work of the Holy Spirit.

Chapter Two

Teaching the Gospel to Children

You might have read or heard about a mother sharing the Gospel with her young son. She mentioned Jesus and letting Him come into his heart. After hearing this, the young boy entered the kitchen and reached into a drawer to pull out a long knife. The child was pointing the knife at his chest when the mother came in and nearly fainted. She screamed, "What are you doing?" The child said that he wanted to let Jesus come into his heart.

As a father, grandfather, and a Sunday school teacher, one thing that I have learned is that children take things literally. <u>Our choice of words is of critical importance as you can see from</u> the above story. What was intended to be a way of having the child accept Jesus "into their heart" nearly became a tragic ending. The child was simply responding to the wording of how the Gospel was presented by his mother. What she was intending to do almost became a tragedy. John MacArthur's book, *A Faith to Grow On,* is one of the finest resources in how to share the Gospel with children that I have ever read.[1]

Children might ask, is Jesus God or is He Man? The answer is both but when I tried to explain this to the children, they could not understand. Here is one way to explain it. When Jesus was born as a human he was 100% Man but He still remained 100% God. How then can He be both 100% God and Man and not add up to 200%? It is always a good idea to read out of the Bible to explain this. In John 1:1, 14 Jesus is called the Word of God. The Word of God *is* Jesus and Jesus *is* the Word of God. He is One and the same. Jesus existed before the beginning of earth and man, and He was with God and the Word (Jesus) was also God (John 1:1). Jesus, as God, also became Man and so He was both God and Man (John 1:14). Now they might wonder how Jesus can be both 100% God and 100% Man. I explain that I am from Kansas so I am 100% Kansan. I was also born in America and so I am also 100% American. I am 100% both however this doesn't add up to 200%. At birth I was both 100% Kansan and 100% American. I am absolutely both and at the same time. I am a legal resident of Kansas and a legal citizen of the United States. There is certainly no conflict in being both. People accept me as both and have no trouble believing this. In like manner, so is Jesus both God and Man. He was referred to as Emanuel in the Old Testament, which simply means "God with us" or God with humans.

Jesus was born as a human but He was never born as a God. He has always been God and He will always be God. He was never created, but has always existed. I *was* created and I did not always exist. So my human example has flaws.

John MacArthur's book looks like it comes from a 3rd grade classroom. The pictures are bright and there are colorful images everywhere. In big, bold lettering come the simplest forms of the message of the Bible. The Bible is a love letter written to humans from the hand of God, as inspired by the Holy Spirit. The Biblical message of salvation has been described as being so deep, an elephant could swim in it, yet so shallow, a child could traverse it.

The most complex things found in the Bible are not in the message of the Gospel itself. The story of salvation through Jesus Christ is made so simple that even a child could understand it and maybe this is why many adults find it too simple and it becomes a major stumbling block for them. Yet, the trust and faith of a child has no problem believing it.

I told my son once that I would be back to pick him up from his grandmas and that I would be there for sure. He had no problem believing this me. He knew I would return. He trusted me enough to know that I would since I had never lied to him before. He cried when I left him but He didn't have to worry that I would forget him because I never did. He wasn't worried that I lied because from experience, he knew that daddy meant what daddy said. He had no trouble believing me. This is the same child-like faith that God desires in all people, children and adults. It's a matter of believing what God has said. That He had planned for Jesus to die for us to take away our sins and that we could live forever with Him. That is not too difficult or abstract to believe. It is concrete in essence especially if they know that God cannot lie. Children have faith and trust unlike most adults do and their faith and trust to a degree, is broader and deeper than that of many adults. Adults tend to be more cynical or skeptical.

When I told my daughter that I would be at her music program, she had complete trust and confidence that I would be there. She accepted it as fact. She never questioned me when I told her something when she way young. She believed what I said because I followed up with what I had promised her. My daughter had complete and full trust in knowing I would do what I said I would do. She knew I was not lying to her. That is exactly what God desires in us and in children – to simply trust and believe Him. It's just easier for children because of their nature. It's no wonder that Jesus emphasizes that unless we become as little children (that is, having a complete and full trust), then "…you will never enter the Kingdom of Heaven"(Matt. 18:3).

I use parts of John MacArthur's book and I make sure our church library has a copy of it. I also like to have Sunday school teachers read it. It presents the Gospel from a child's point of view. Having the perspective of a child is important. When I worked for Head Start as a Regional Manger as the Early Childhood Educational Manager, I got down on my knees and "walked" around the room at our Head Start centers. This allowed me to have the same perspective that the children would have in their classrooms. This enabled me to see if shelves where too high to access books, toys or manipulatives. I especially looked for heavier items on top shelves to prevent a child from pulling something down onto themselves and causing injury. I checked electrical cords and outlets. I looked for carpet threads that could be pulled out and swallowed. My first concern was for the child and not the convenience of the teacher. This is the same perspective John MacArthur takes in his book *A Faith to Grow On* and it is the perspective I always try to emulate in the classroom and in fact, with new believers. It simplifies the plan of God and the message of the Bible, starting from the beginning to Jesus ascension.

In Chapter One it talks about God as the Creator and where everything, including people, came from. It discusses the fact that God is spirit and we cannot see him, just like the wind (p. 12). You can't see the wind, but you can see its effect. This chapter discusses the ways that we are like God and ways in which we are not like Him (p. 14). The book speaks about how God has lived forever and will live forever, even though that is a hard concept even for adults to grasp. Chapters Three and Four tell how our sin has separated us from God but that God was not caught by surprise and already planned a way for us to go to heaven (p. 62). Jesus planned to take our punishment on Himself and pay a penalty that we could never pay ourselves (p. 64).

Chapter Four discusses the fact that God is invisible but He does talk to us in His book that He wrote and gave to us [the Bible] (p. 72). God doesn't want any of us to be separated from Him (p. 88) and so this is why God planned for Jesus to come down from Heaven and live a perfect, sinless life too to make this possible (p. 90). Since Jesus never sinned, He obeyed in our place (2 Cor 5:21). The Father wanted Jesus to pay a penalty that would let us live with Him – meaning that we would never die. Jesus did this on purpose (p. 92). That is how much He loved us (John 3:16). Jesus proved that we could live again after we died because *He* did (p. 96).

In Chapter Six, we know that anything we will ever do wrong can be forgiven and we will be made perfect some day because of what Jesus did (p. 104). This is the reason that we need to be thankful to God for how much He sacrificed for us (p. 110). He owned everything in the universe but He wants to share it with us (p. 114). That's why we sing songs of how great He is in church, at home or in the car. You can't keep any secrets from God like you can from your parents or your friends because God even knows what you're thinking (p. 116).

Chapter Eight says that we can talk to Him in prayer. This is like asking your parents for something and just telling them what you want (p. 124). You know God cannot give you everything you want because He knows, like your parents, that some things will hurt us. God, like your parents, knows what you need and knows what is best for you better than you or your parents do. You can know that God will never give you anything that is not good for you. He wants to give you what you *need* but not always what you want, because what you want might end up hurting you.

In Chapter Nine, John MacArthur talks about the church. The church is not the building but the people, just like a house is not the family (p. 142). The reason we go to church is for us to work together and help other people get to know Jesus (p. 144). This is one of the reasons why we need to be nice to people and forgive them, because God forgives us - if we ask for it (p. 152). God wants us to forgive the bullies, the people who push us, the mean children, and even the ones who cheat (p. 156).

In Chapters Eleven and Twelve, children are told why we should share this news with other people. If you knew something that was so wonderful, wouldn't you want to tell your friends, your grandparents, or your neighbors (p. 164)? Don't be surprised if people don't like you if you tell them about Jesus, because they hated Jesus when He talked about God (p. 168).

The final chapter presents the gospel so well. It says that we just have to believe in and trust Jesus and know that He died for us so that we can live forever with Him (p. 178). It is possible to trust Jesus because He is perfect and He never lies – He always speaks the truth (p. 180). They can go to heaven – and it is *the* most wonderful place there is (p. 186).

To believe in Jesus is not letting Him come into your heart, repeating a sinner's prayer, filling out a decision card, or walking down the aisle. To believe in Jesus means that they can believe in Him, they can fully trust Him, they can absolutely rely upon Him, and they can have a full assurance that He will completely keep His word and save them. The fact is Jesus wants you to be with Him forever and He can make sure you live forever.

When my daughter asked about this, we were surprised. It caught us off guard. We never forced her into it or never tried to talk her into it. My wife and I never saw it coming. That is the way it should be. It is the *child's* decision. God does the calling - we do not. It is not our responsibility – it is *their* response to *His* ability – but it is *our* responsibility to tell them about Him. A forced conversion is not a real conversion – that is a caving into parental pressure. This is not how God calls people. He never forces Himself on anyone. Getting saved is *always* up to the person, child or adult, and is from God alone (John 6:44).

I recommend this book to any parent, Sunday school teacher, grandparent or anyone that is the caregiver. It presents the Gospel in such a clear way that it works well with adults too. To be saved one must repent of their sins (even a child can understand – when they are *ready*), confess them to God, see their need for Jesus to save them, and then put their trust in Him.

For more on this, read Romans 10:9-13.

---

1. John MacArthur. *A Faith to Grow On.* Thomas Nelson, Inc., Nashville, Tenn. Copyright 2000. ISBN 0-8-499-7512-3

John Mac Arthur is founder of Grace to You Ministries. www.gty.org

Chapter Three

Become As Little Children

Children are a gift of God. Children take things literally. In this chapter you will read of two events that show we must exercise great care in *how* we share the Gospel with young children. This lady I know had company come over and her young child of five came into the living room and told the lady who was visiting, that "Momma was right...you like to talk a lot!" Ouch! Oh well, out of the mouth of babes they say. Children are brutally honest, right? I prefer to say they are refreshingly honest. When children are young there is a precious window of opportunity where many children come to trust in Jesus and I have seen from experience that this prime time of their lives is perhaps the best opportunity for us to tell them the message of the Gospel. With this time comes a serious consideration for caregivers to watch carefully what they say around or to children.

One of my favorite verses is "And He called a little child to Himself and put him in the midst of the, and said, 'Truly I say to you, unless you repent (change, turn around) and become like little children (trusting, loving, humble), you can never enter the kingdom of heaven (at all). Whoever will humble himself therefore and become like this little child is the greatest in the kingdom of heaven'" (Matt. 18:2-4). These true stories I will share made me realize that there is much more in presenting the Gospel to children than I had ever thought. These two stories forever changed the way in which I would talk about the story of salvation through Jesus Christ.

The first event I mentioned earlier in this book and it stunned me because I realized that our words have a great impact on children. A young child's mother had been sharing the good news about Jesus Christ and how people go to heaven. The child was told that his mother had already believed in Jesus Christ and was assured of going to heaven. Perhaps he was troubled and didn't want to be separated from her. The child also wanted to go to heaven, so he asked his mother how he could go to there too. The mother said that "You must let Jesus come into your heart to live, and then He will live in your heart forever." Moments later, the child went into the kitchen and when the mother heard the silverware drawer open, she was curious what the child was up to. She nearly fainted when she saw the young boy with a knife in his hand, pointed at his chest. She rushed to the boy and grabbed the knife and asked him, what are you doing? The young boy said that he was going to let Jesus come into his heart. The boy thought he had to literally cut his heart open to allow Jesus' room to come in.

This true story made me realize the way in which we share the Gospel must be in very specific, precise language. For the child, he was only doing what he thought he had to do to make room for Jesus to come into his heart. He thought that he had to make an opening for Jesus to be able to come into his heart and live inside it.

Another touching true story was about a young boy. This boy showed the trusting faith and deep love that is unconditional in children. He knew that his older sister was very sick and she needed to receive a blood transfusion very soon and since her blood type was extremely rare, only her brother's blood type would help. The boy's father asked him if they could use his blood to help his sister. The boy thought for just a few seconds and then, said yes. When the boy was lying down next to his sister and seeing his blood being removed from his body and being transferred to a machine that was used for his sister, tears started coming out of his eyes. His parents seeing the boy's tears asked if he was okay. The boy asked his parents, "Will I see you in heaven?" The father said, "Yes, son, some day." The boy said, "I will miss you." His father said, "Son you're not going to heaven now." The boy then said, "I thought you died when your blood is gone." It was then that the father realized that his son thought he was going to give *all* of his blood to his sister and then die. After hearing this, both of parents began crying and the father said, "Son, you're not going to die...they are only going to take *some* of your blood."

The boy understood that once all of his blood was gone that he would die, yet he still willingly gave his blood to save his sister and please his parents. This was the reason that the boy hesitated for a while when the parents had asked him if he could give his blood to help his sister. Not knowing the fact that the boy would only have to give *some* of his blood, and thinking that he was going to give *all* of his blood, he was still willing to give it – and to die for his sister. The boy naturally thought that once all of his blood was gone that he would die and that explained why he cried silently while he gave some his blood. He was thinking that he wouldn't see his family for a long time – and that is the reason why he had asked them if he would see them in heaven. The boy was *still* willing to give his life for his sister but he wanted to make sure that he would see them in heaven someday.

How touching and how very precious is the unconditional love of children – and this boy in particular. This boy had a child-like faith and trust in his parents who had told him that if he believed in and had faith in Jesus Christ, that he would go to heaven. That is why Jesus said that we have to have this same child-like trust, faith, and belief in Him in order to be saved. That type of love is close to Jesus' unconditional love for us. He has such a passionate desire to save us that He died for us. Likewise, we must come to Jesus in humble obedience, repentance, trust, and believe in Him. The way in which we share the Gospel with children involves the faith and trust that the boy had – we believe in the only One Who can save. Believe in Him and anyone can be saved (Acts 16:30-31). Once a person is saved they can be sure that they will stay saved (John 6:37, 29, 10:28-29). He never breaks His promise. It's not what *we* do, but what *He* has done (John 3:16). Any that come to Him as a little child in complete trust, faith, and full assurance will be saved (Acts 4:12, Matt 18:2-4).

Chapter Four

What Is the Age of Accountability?

Do Babies Go To Heaven?

What is the point of including in this book a chapter addressing the question of where babies go if they die? For certain it is one of the single most difficult experiences for any human being to go through. The Bible does not give a precise age of accountability and there is no scriptural reference or evidence of a particular age of its being too late or early for a person to trust in the Lord Jesus Christ as Savior. There appears to be a special dispensation of God's mercy given to those who are very young and this is the specific focus of this chapter.

After a baby dies, where do they go? What about the unborn, the still-born, aborted fetuses, young children and even special needs children or adults? What about those who are severely mentally handicapped or those with serious mental diseases or disorders? Are they held responsible if they die prematurely? What about adults with severely limited mental capacities? Are they held responsible since they have not trusted in Jesus Christ as Savior? Are they held responsible since only those who believe in Jesus are saved (Acts 16:30-31)? Where do these, so young and tender, go after death? Is there any hope for someone who has lost one so precious? Are there any promises in the Bible about their fate? What does the Word of God say about them? What can we tell someone who has lost one of these young ones or those who have special needs or severe mental retardation? What does the Bible say is their final destination?

Children are an extension of us and they are our future. When someone loses an infant, a young child or a baby, it is absolutely devastating. It is like part of them has died. It's even more tragic when it is one that is so young who had their whole life ahead of them. They missed out on so much love to both give and to receive. The future hopes of weddings, graduations, Christmas mornings, grandma and grandpa are all gone, forever. Or is it? I believe that the fate of these precious, departed ones is an important issue for any parent, grandparent, foster parent, or caregiver. Perhaps we can find answers in the Bible because God the Father knows something about losing a Son.

We do know that no one can be saved without having placed their faith in Jesus Christ (Acts 4:12). If there is no Savior there can be no eternal life. We *do* know that God cares about what happens to infants, fetuses, or even young children the moment they die. If God cares for the sparrow that falls to the ground, He surely cares for children – most certainly about those who have been aborted. God has said that all humans are born into sin but surely babies are not condemned are they?

Sometimes saying nothing is the best thing that you can do with a grieving parent. What can be said to help in such a situation anyway? Just sitting with them in silence and grieving quietly with them is the only thing that we can do. The worst thing to say is "I understand what you are going through" or "Keep a stiff upper lip." We cannot know what they are going through if we haven't been through it ourselves. Only they know the depths of loss that they are experiencing at the moment. Is there anything in the Bible that might provide us with some words of hope and comfort about their great loss? There really is nothing you can say, except "I'm so sorry" because no one but them can really understand what this is like. Grieve with them, cry with them, and express your sorrow for their loss. And that's all that anyone can really do.

Today, many Christians and non-Christians alike can carry a heavy burden of guilt and shame after an abortion, lingering throughout their entire life. Despite the fact that God forgave someone who committed murder, conspiracy to commit murder, and adultery, (King David), they cannot forgive themselves but God is more than willing. The good news is that there is nothing that God cannot forgive. The only real unpardonable sin is not repenting and trusting in Christ as Savior.

If we depend upon the Word of God and it is in the Bible, then we can definitively know for certain and we don't have to depend on human opinions. The Bible can provide answers to particular issues and so we *can* know for certain.

It is hard to believe, but *some* Christians think aborted fetuses, babies or young children who die do not go to heaven. They reason that anyone who does not trust in Christ is headed straight to hell or they cease to exist but that is not biblical. There is nothing anywhere in the Bible that indicates that. God is God and only The Almighty is qualified to say, "I will have mercy upon whom I will have mercy." The good news is that most Christians don't believe that babies go to hell. Theological traditions hold that those children who die in infancy are numbered among the redeemed. That is to say, they have a certain level of confidence that God will be particularly gracious toward those who have never had the opportunity to be exposed to the Gospel, such as children, infants, and even fetuses that were aborted either intentionally or by miscarriage.

Adult men and women have no excuse before God because they know better (Rom. 1:19-20), but babies cannot believe in what they do not know, and therefore cannot be held responsible. Jesus always accepts children and He indicates that in the New Testament several times. This was even found in the Old Testament when God refused to let the disobedient Israelites enter the Promised Land due to their unbelief, however, He did not hold the children responsible for what their parents have done. God says in Deuteronomy 1:39 that "your little ones...your children, which in that day had no knowledge between good and evil, they shall go into it, and to them will I give it, and they will possess it."

When the people were bringing their children to Jesus to be touched by him, His disciples rebuked them, but Jesus saw this and was angry. He said, "Suffer the little children to come unto me, and forbid them not: for of such is the kingdom of God. (Mark 10:14)" Just look at Kind David's example of children not being accountable for their salvation in the event that they should die. King David, after having lost his infant child, declared in full confidence that he would most certainly see his child again, saying "He cannot come to me, but I can go to him" (2 Sam 12:23). God also plainly declares that "<u>Before I formed you in the womb I knew you; before you were born I set you apart</u>" (Jer. 1:5).

Matthew 22:32 Jesus said that, "He (God) is not the God of the dead but of the living." My wife, after conception of our child, stroked, patted, sang, and softly spoke to our unborn child. We both already loved this baby, even though she was not yet born and not even knowing she was a *she* yet! Similarly, God knew us and loved us, even before the time that we were conceived. In Psalm 139:13-16 He says, "For you created my inmost being; you knit me together in my mother's womb. I praise you because I am fearfully and wonderfully made; your works are wonderful, I know that full well. My frame was not hidden from you when I was made in the secret place. When I was woven together in the depths of the earth, your eyes saw my unformed body. All the days ordained for me were written in your book before one of them came to be." In fact, "he chose us in himself before the creation of the world to be holy and blameless in his sight. In love he predestined us for adoption to sonship through Jesus Christ, in accordance with his pleasure and will" (Eph 1:4-5).

Now, what about the severely mentally retarded or the severely disabled including adult or those who remain in a vegetative state from youth into adulthood and those who cannot perhaps be reached for whatever reason like for example autism? Again, there is nothing in the Bible that indicates that God's dispensation of grace for those who are so encumbered that they are not able to trust in Jesus will be held against them. Jesus went right up to the "mentally violent" and caste out their demons, so He must realize that salvation is not possible without a mental capacity to understand it so those with special needs who have no chance in this present life will surely have a chance in the "new heavens and new earth" that Peter mentions (2 Pet 3:13). <u>Nothing can prevent God's dispensation of grace</u> (death, handicaps, etc.). The only thing that would prevent someone from being saved or lost would be that they are not old enough or able to understand repentance and trust in Christ.

As soon as God entered into a relationship with Abraham, he brought Isaac into it—when Isaac was still an infant and didn't have an understanding of what was going on. God in fact knew *before* Isaac was even born and before he was even a fetus. We also see David's situation in the Old Testament when his infant child dies. David is fully confident that he will see his child again. The story of David and Bathsheba's infant dying gives tremendous consolation to parents who have lost infants or young children to death, or to miscarriages. We are not the ones to determine who God will have mercy on.

The point is that infants who die are believed to be given a special dispensation of the grace of God; it is not by their innocence but by God's grace that they are received unto Himself. There are great controversies that hover over the doctrine of original sin. Lutherans disagree with Roman Catholics, who disagree in turn with Presbyterians, etc., on the scope and extent of what we call original sin. <u>Understand that the original sin does not refer to the first sin that was committed, but rather to the result of that fall, the entrance of sin into the world,</u> so that all of us are born in a fallen state. We come into this world with a sin nature, and so the baby that dies will die as a sinful child and when that child is received by God, he or she is received by grace.

We come into this world with a sin nature, and so the baby that dies will die in a state of sin but when that child is received by God, he or she is received by grace. You may rest assured because God would not exclude others something that He has done for David.

When David and Bathsheba lost their precious child, David realized that he could not expect to see him again in this life, but he clearly said the day will come when "I shall go to him..." (2 Sam 12:23). Interestingly, in the very next verse it is said that, "David comforted Bathsheba his wife" (V. 24) with this same assurance that they would see the child again. This belief was just as common then as it is today. And what a joyous reunion that will be!

There really is no age of accountability mentioned in the Bible. For some it may be early, for others it may come in the teen years and who knows, it may be into early adulthood or beyond. We just don't know. God is silent on the specific age of accountability so I will be too. Just as soon as a person understands repentance, confession, sin, and trusting in Christ, then they can comprehend what salvation is and be saved or refuse it, but no human knows exactly when that age is. God alone is sovereign in determining when a person is accountable to receive the Gospel and deemed to be beyond that age. This privileged information is God's alone because "The secret things belong to the LORD our God, but the things revealed belong to us and to our children forever" (Duet 29:29). No human can make this determination however if you or someone you know has lost a loved one, young or old, that reunion will not happen if you have not repented and trusted in Jesus Christ as Savior.

I pray that you would pass this on to anyone who has ever dealt with such a heartbreaking issue such as losing a baby, infant, fetus, or young child or has a severely mentally disabled child, no matter the age. I also hope this provides healing for whoever has ever carried around this heavy yoke of guilt and shame from having an abortion and comforts those who have lost someone so precious and young. Put all of this on His broad shoulders. Take His yoke and lay all your burdens upon Him. The child will yet live again.

Chapter Five

The Three Types of Parents

There are ways to effectively coach your children in life. This includes coaching them at home, school and of last importance, in sports. <u>Words of encouragement go a long way in making them more effective in these areas of</u> life. There are primarily three types of parents: The Drill Sergeant, the Search and Rescuer, and the Consultant. Which type of parent are you?

The Drill Sergeant is the type of parent that is always in the face of the child and is constantly pushing and pressuring them to do better at home and in school. Even in sports, they can be yelling at their children to their extreme embarrassment. Saying, or perhaps, yelling at them to "clean up your room" or "get your homework done or no supper for you!" They may get these things done, but it is often associated with provoking them to anger or they do it out of fear. In this way, there is no internal locus of control built; just a "my way or the highway" mentality.

What they learn is if they want other people to do things for them, the way get it done is through shouting or intimidating others. This pattern for getting things accomplished will likely be repeated in their own children's lives someday. A vicious cycle is established and one that will not easily be broken, but can be repeated, generation after generation.

The Search and Rescuer parent is the type of parent that constantly hovers over a child waiting for a mistake; not to yell at them, but to drop in and rescue them. This type of parent wants to rescue them from something that the parent deems the child is not capable of doing for themselves. This builds an externally-dependent child. A child, who when they experience difficulty, will often give up in frustration because they realize that they cannot do it, determined by the parent that always comes to the rescue.

An important lesson is never learned by the child - that is through trial and error they can actually discover how to solve problems on their own. What happens when the day comes, and it *will* come, when the child leaves home and has to do for themselves? This type of child tends to be fearful of challenges and change and may actually be thwarted by life's ups and downs. If they learn anything, it is that they cannot learn nor do anything on their own. They learn to depend on the parents or others for things that, given the chance, they could actually learn to do for themselves, therefore, their life is always limited by what they deem is impossible because they have been rescued so many times that they are unable to accomplish difficult tasks.

The Consultant is the type of parent that is neither a Drill Sergeant or a Search and Rescuer. They let the child try to establish for themselves how they can solve problems. They allow the child to try and fail only to try again, eventually to succeed. When things get frustrating for a child, the parent does not try to do it for them or they don't try to yell or scream them into submission. The parent acts as a consultant. The consultant parent might approach a child who is going through a difficult assignment like this: "Wow, I see that you are really having difficulties. I remember when I was your age and I had problems with math too. I just had to go to the back of the textbook and look at several examples to see how they solved these equations. I don't know what you're going to do, but that's what *I* did. Let me know if I can help you in anyway."

There seems to be a correlation between letting children solve their own problems and when they ask for help, being there for them. Cheering them on when they have success while being sympathetic and consulting when they have difficulties. Positive reinforcement and allowing a child to fail is a productive way for teaching children to learn how to solve problems on their own and to ask for help when they need it. Then you can cheer them on when they *do* succeed. It takes ten positive comments to make up for one negative one and being sympathetic and consulting is always more productive in the long term, than yelling or doing it for them.

Chapter Six

How to Talk Your Children about Sex

When do you bring up the topic of sex to your children? How do you talk to your children about sex? What should you tell them is the purpose of sex? What things should be spoken of from the Bible? What happens if you don't bring up sex to children?

You really bring up sex when you treat your wife or husband in a loving way. When a relation between the father and mother is a loving, caring, and affectionate one, then you have already brought up sex in one way. Children will learn to treat the opposite sex the way that they see their father or mother treated. They will see this as normal and their expectations of the opposite sex will be primarily based upon the relationship that they see between their father and mother. It has been said that children cannot hear what you say to them because what you are doing is drowning it out. Actions do speak louder than words, so this important reminder for all parents should be; they are watching, they are learning and more is caught than taught.

When parents first bring up the topic of sex they might bring up an example of the birds and the bees. The fact is that using the animal kingdom is a great way to bring up the subject. You could note that the young birds are best taken care of by parent birds. They provide food, shelter, and protection for the young nestlings. Now if there were not two to care for the young, then the young birds might starve, or have no shelter, or might not be adequately protected. Birds generally mate for life and they do not have young by themselves. It takes two to raise the nestlings. It is not a job for a lone, single bird to do and this might be a great lesson to know that having children requires a man and a woman to become husband and wife because nature teaches us that it takes both parents to raise children and that is the way that God intended it to be.

The topic of sex should be brought up as soon as possible so that the embarrassment is taken out of the subject. Your children should have a safe-zone feeling where they can bring up anything or ask any question of their parents. Parents should not look or act uncomfortable when sex is brought up and it will definitely come up with all the media emphasis on it today. No question should be rejected or treated as unimportant. Parents wouldn't you much rather have your children come to you about such things than to have them learn it from other children or from the street?

Here should be the time to discuss the proper touching and where certain areas of their body are that are private even from mommy and daddy. Children should have a clear understanding of what is permissible and what is not and to have no fear in approaching the parent anytime that they feel uncomfortable about an occurrence where they were touched in a "private" area. Tell them that some adults lie about things like touching them in private areas and if they do tell anyone, they will harm their parents. Tell them that they will never be in any trouble if they come to them about such things and that no matter what anyone says or whatever kinds of threats they make, nobody can touch them in private areas, even if it's a daddy, mommy, grandma or grandpa, an uncle or aunt…anybody at all, ever!

How do you Talk to Your Children about Sex?

When you do talk to children about sex, insist that it is *only* for adults that are married and never for children or adults that are not married. Warn them that it's bad for them to expose themselves or for someone to show their private areas to them and especially to have touch them in a private area and for them to do the same thing, even if someone tells them that it's okay. Sex is a good thing because is a gift from God but it is only for daddies and mommies. Tell them that God does not want them to have any relations where they feel it is not right. If it doesn't feel right to them, then it is probably wrong. They should feel free to talk to talk to you at any time about anything or if they have any questions.

Sex should be something that is only for those who are married and it is always between adults. No children, young adults, or even older adults are supposed to be touching or be touched or to see or be seen by anyone else unless they are married; and only then by the person that they are married to. When my children were young, I always accompanied them to visits to the pediatrician. If any pediatrician forbids me or my wife from being present for any procedure or examination, we would find another pediatrician.

Talking about sex being a good thing and that is how children are born is a necessary part of growing up but it is always, and there are no exceptions, between a married man and woman. You can tell them that without sex, they would not have been born. Sex is for married couples only and God created sex for married adults. He did not make it for anyone that was not married but only for men and women who were married and is never for children. Even sex between men and sex between women is something you can tell them that God does not approve of and it is disobeying God for He didn't create sex for that purpose.

What Should You Tell Them is the Purpose of Sex?

Some of this was discussed in the previous section. Sex is for the purpose of having children and that sex is purposely intended for mommies and daddies that are married to each other. Sex is a special thing and it should never, ever be shared outside of marriage. Tell them that someday, when they get married, they will have children of your own. This is the only time that God allows sex. It is a special thing that God made for married people. It was never meant for anyone that is not married and it can harm people in a way that their lives may never be the same.

What Things Should Be Spoken of from the Bible?

I once heard a young boy and girl were being married by a little girl who was performing the ceremony. The little girl's ceremony went like this:

The little girl: "Do you take this man for better or for worse?"

The young girl: "For better!"

The little girl: "Do you take him in sickness or health?"

The young girl: "In health!"

The little girl: "Do you take him for richer or poorer?"

The young girl: "For richer!"

This was quite funny but you can always read them the account of the story from Genesis chapter one where God joined together the man and woman, Adam and Eve. You may emphasize that God is the one that joins them together and that they are made to stay married for the rest of their lives.

You may also tell them that God doesn't like it when daddies and mommies leave each other because this hurts the family. It also hurts the children. Of course, if you had to divorce a spouse because they left the marriage, or they were unfaithful, or they were abusive, then you can tell them that God allows daddies and mommies to live in different houses if it is the best thing for the family. The parent's job is to protect the children and this is what God wants the parents to do.

What Happens If You Don't Bring Up Sex to Children?

I never knew my father and I lived with my aunt for a long time and no one ever talked about sex, so we learned about sex from our friends and from the playground (or the street). It seemed that it was always wrong too. I remember being told in the 1st grade that if I kissed a girl they would have a baby…needless to say I was terrified for a long time to even touch a girl, not to mention kiss one. When my aunt would kiss me, it horrified me because I didn't understand. So talk to your children about sex when they are old enough to understand. Even when they are young they should understand about being touched in private areas and that no one, not even their relatives which include mommy and daddy, has the right to touch them in their private areas even with their clothes on.

If you don't talk to them about sex, without embarrassment and without putting them off, they will learn about it one way or another. As in my case, it will usually be wrong. There is never a question that your children should be afraid or embarrassed to ask you. Tell them that. That safe-zone builds trust and provides an environment where they can come to you about anything and that is the best of situations; especially when they come to you about sex.

Chapter Seven

How to Discipline Children in Love

Is Spanking Biblical?

Should Christians spank their young children? Is it biblical to discipline in such a way? What principles can we learn from the Bible as to whether spanking is what God would want parents to do?

Discipline and Not Abuse

There has never been more disagreement between non-believers and Christians and even among Christians themselves than over the issue of whether parents should spank their children or not. Disciplining a child is not child abuse and spanking is never to be done in anger or in a fit of rage. The parent needs to cool off before they do or even say anything. Parents of a strong-willed child feel it necessary to spank young children to prevent them from doing serious harm to themselves or endangering their lives. To catch a child in the early stages of dangerous activity is important because it sends a strong message to the child who is old enough to understand that they will have certain consequences for particular actions. Older children may be better off by giving them a time out or adolescents or teenagers can be disciplined by restricting their Internet, video games, or cell phone usage.

The type of discipline very much depends upon the age and the understanding of the child. Every child needs discipline but so do adults but God sees to that. Young children may have to have discipline if they disobey direct parental orders that they can clearly understand. Keeping them in an environment so strictly controlled can disrupt natural activities of the remaining members of the household and may not always be practical or possible. In other words, children must have some freedom and not be in lock-down all the time and since they need some freedom, the will necessarily make poor choices. That is part of growing up. Even a child that plays outside in a fenced area can find ways to harm themselves. One parent I knew had to discipline his young toddler because he kept eating flowers from the flower bed. It was not practical to get rid of all the flowers in the flower bed but some flowers can be poisonous to children. There must be supervision of course but children can be very sneaky and can find ways to get into all kinds of trouble or serious danger and in a very short amount of time!

Spare the Rod, Spoil the Child

This saying "spare the rod and spoil the child" has truth to it but it has been corrupted more than any other by non-believers because they see it as the Bible teaching Christian parents that it's okay to use a rod for correction on their children. Nothing could be further from the truth. In the first place, this is twisting the actual Bible verse from its context which says "Whoever spares the rod hates his son, but he who loves him is diligent to discipline him" (Prov 13:24. One thing that most translations do not bring out in this verse is that it should read "Whoever spares the rod hates his son, but he who loves him "disciplines him early." That is the proper interpretation. The key is to discipline children early before their character is solidly grounded and harder to change. The "rod" that people emphasize is not an actual rod but it is symbolic of the parent's corrective discipline. Proverbs 13:24 is not explicitly saying that corporal punishment (spanking) is commanded but it doesn't exclude this option either. Each parent must make that decision for themselves.

Some states have stricter laws than others and it may be criminal to spank in public in one state while it is not in another. If spanking is done, as with all discipline, it should be done in private so as not to humiliate the child in public. How would an adult like to be taken to task in public? Not likely. When dealing with a stubborn three-year-old that refuses to be disciplined by time outs or withholding certain privileges, parents may see spanking as the only option. I will neither recommend nor try to discourage spanking. That is a choice each parent must make with their own children because each child is different and differing methods of discipline may be more effective and work much better than spanking. There are always alternative methods to spanking that a parent could use and spanking should not be considered the first or only option of discipline. Sometimes children can do things so quickly and it's impossible to watch them ever single second of the day. In only takes a split-and they can suddenly be in harm's way. Parents know their children better than anyone else so no one expert can tell you exactly what to do.

Real Child Abuse

Child abuse is illegal of course. Never strike a child when anger. Take a time out before you do something you will regret. Children are much more vulnerable to injury than adults are. You can be arrested and lose custody of your children for child abuse but I do not believe that spanking and child abuse are the same thing. It can be, but that is where parents need to be careful and not discipline a child in anger.

The other extreme is also child abuse. That is parental neglect. The parents neglecting to discipline a child is an alternate form of child abuse. The opposite of love is not hate...it is indifference or apathy. To let a child do what they want is to show the child that no rules or no law's is a good thing. To "spare the rod"...or spare correction...is to spoil the child. The Proverb is true that "a child left undisciplined disgraces its mother" (29:15) because even "the LORD disciplines those he loves, as a father the son he delights in" (Prov 3:12).

Conclusion

Love equals discipline; no discipline is equal to not loving them. Love and discipline go hand in hand. You can't have love without discipline. You must "Discipline your children, for in that there is hope; do not be a willing party to their death" (Prov 19:18) because "Folly is bound up in the heart of a child, but the rod of discipline will drive it far away" (Prov 22:15) and so "Do not withhold discipline from a child; if you punish them with the rod, they will not die" (Prov 23:13). Children, parents are not off the hook either because God tells us that He lovingly disciplines us too:

"My son, do not regard lightly the discipline of the Lord, nor be weary when reproved by him. For the Lord disciplines the one he loves and chastises every son whom he receives." It is for discipline that you have to endure. God is treating you as sons. For what son is there whom his father does not discipline? If you are left without discipline, in which all have participated, then you are illegitimate children and not sons. Besides this, we have had earthly fathers who disciplined us and we respected them. Shall we not much more be subject to the Father of spirits and live? For they disciplined us for a short time as it seemed best to them, but he disciplines us for our good, that we may share his holiness. For the moment all discipline seems painful rather than pleasant, but later it yields the peaceful fruit of righteousness to those who have been trained by it" (Heb 12:5-11).

Chapter Eight

How to Keep Children from Leaving the Church

The Disappearing Youth

As a former Sunday school teacher of some twenty years, I have seen more and more of these children go off to college and fall away from their belief in God. First of all, the national divorce rate for people who regularly attend church is about the same as those who do not – roughly 50% so it would appear that church members are becoming more and more like the world. Secondly, two out of three high school kids coming from Evangelical homes that go off to college are agnostic or atheistic by the time they graduate.

Since the youth of today are the future but also the present part of the church, the more youth that fall away in disbelief, the less they are there to replace those who are older in the faith as they age and either passes away or goes into nursing homes or assisted living centers. There is no replacement of membership to fill in those who are becoming too old to attend or are becoming shut-ins so that is having the effect of dwindling attendance numbers in churches. It also hasn't helped that in the past 20 years the number of American people who say they have no religion has doubled and has now reached 15 percent. Those numbers are concentrated in the under-30 population. The polling data continues to show that a dramatic exit is taking place from American Christian churches. The Barna Group, a leading research organization focusing on the intersection of faith and culture, reported in 2012 that 80 percent of the young people raised in a church will be "disengaged" before they are 30. This is perhaps the biggest reason that so many churches are losing membership in America.

The Opposite of Love

If you are a parent, you discipline your child because you love them. If you saw them out in the street playing and they refused to get out of the street, you'd likely discipline them because you don't want them to be hurt or killed. The reason is that you love your children. If you saw a blind man headed toward a cliff you'd very likely warn them that they are in grave danger of falling off the cliff and either being badly hurt or even killed, wouldn't you? I would think most of us would. Here is the key thing about love then. The opposite of love is not hate; it is apathy or indifference.

If you saw your children in mortal danger and didn't care enough about them or love them enough to warn them or rescue them, then you couldn't say that you really loved them. You'd let them be hurt or killed because you lacked a love that would motivate you to do something; anything you could to save them. The same thing applies to the blind man headed for the cliff. If you really didn't love people or care for them at all, then you'd be apathetic toward what was about to happen to them and instead of going to them and warning them, you'd just sit by and watch or even turn away. Hate is not the opposite of love because if there is hate, there is at least some feeling there because if you were completely apathetic then you'd have no reason to hate; you wouldn't care at all.

4 Traits of Youth Who Don't Leave the Church

What are some traits that parents or foster parents, and even grandparents can look for in youths that don't leave the church?

True Conversion

The most important trait of all for the youth that don't leave the church is that they were born again because they were equipped and fed the Word of God and not simply entertained. In most cases, their parents have been both preaching the gospel and living it out and were not being hypocrites; that is they weren't saying one thing and living the opposite way. Young people can see through hypocrisy a mile away and when they see phoniness, they want nothing to do with it because they don't want to live a life of duplicity and who could blame them. Generally speaking, converted youth stay in the church, just like converted older adults.

They are Involved

If you include children in the different ministries of the church, they'll more like "buy in" to the church and what the church is doing. For some reason, almost 90% of the youth leave the church today once they're out of school or go into college and move away from home. The world beats them down, the secularist professors shame them down, and the lusts of the flesh pull them down. I know when I went to college the temptations went through the roof. The availability of sinful activities was overwhelming. I am certain it's even worse for today's youth out in the world but if you keep them connected by serving in some capacities in church ministries, they are more likely to want to continue that. I had a young lady who was our elder's daughter. She got involved with a nursing home ministry and visitation I started and the residents loved her and she, in turn, began loving them. She didn't want to give that wonderful feeling of serving up and it kept her connected to the church, even when she got older.

They Become Teachers

Some of our best Sunday school substitutes and Sunday school teachers were the youth. When these young adults feel needed by the younger children such as in serving as teachers, assisting the Sunday school teacher, or being a substitute Sunday school teacher, they stick to their home church because they don't want to let their students or these young children down. I tried to mentor a young man to take over for me someday for Sunday school in my class of $3^{rd}/4^{th}$ grade combined. I started giving him more and more responsibility. I allowed him freedom and to make mistakes without being a mother hen to him. Today, he's one of the best Sunday school teachers there is in the church.

Mentoring

I strongly believe that every Timothy needs a Paul and every Paul needs to mentor a young Timothy but the same applies to both young men and women. That's why Paul said "Older women likewise are to be reverent in their behavior, not malicious gossips nor enslaved to much wine, teaching what is good" (Titus 2:3) and "urge the young men to be sensible; in all things show yourself to be an example of good deeds, with purity in doctrine, dignified" (Titus 2:6-7). When youth have great role models in the church and some of these role models are mentoring the youth, these youth are more likely to stay. I tell these young people that they will have to mentor someone someday to take their place. I want them to think of the future and make sure they know that they're being role models today for those who will be the younger generation tomorrow and the church will need them to mentor the generation that follows them.

6 Things You Should Never Say To Your Child

Every parent has regretted saying things to their child. What 6 things should you never say to your child? What things would you include?

You'll Never Amount to Anything

I have heard people that actually heard this from their parents and they never got over it and even though they did amount to something significant in their life, these words penetrated into the deepest inner recesses of their mind and heart. They left a long lasting wound that is still there today and like a scar, it's a permanent reminder.

You Never/You Always

No one always does the one thing or never does one thing in particular so avoid saying "You never" (fill in the blank) or "You always" (whatever it is). If you're not careful, it could be a self-fulfilling prophecy. For example, if you tell your child enough times that they never clean up their room, why would they want to? If you tell them that they always fail at math, then they'll give up trying. It becomes what is called a self-fulfilling prophecy where you expect them to always or never do this or that and they'll live up/or down to that expectation. Never make sweeping statements like you never do this or you always do that because that is never true.

You're a Bad boy/Bad girl

This one really hurts deep. I think it is always best to separate the actions from the child. In other words, if they make a bad choice tell them that they made a bad decision or choice, never that they are a bad child. They will begin to believe it if they hear it often enough and will have little or no motivation to ever want to change. You're just like your father/mother/sister/brother

This one brings a person down but it also brings or puts down the person that you're associating them with. What if your mother said "You're just like your father" or you father said "You're just like your mother." That would certainly hurt them but it would also make them angry because even though their mother or father's not perfect, it's their mother and father and you're putting them down too. When you say "You're just like" you're locking them into a stereotype and making it impossible for them to escape from it.

You Never Do Anything Right

This one is close to "You always" and "You never" but it's a bit different. By saying this, you make them think that everything they do or will ever do will be wrong and we all know that's not true. This is such a destructive sentence because it not only destroys morale for the moment but it makes the future seem pointless and so they feel it's useless to even try anymore.

I'm Through With You/I Wished I Never Had Kids

I combined these two because so often they go together. It could also be stated as "I give up on you" and this would make the child believe that they can never go to you for advice or counsel. This almost makes the child seem that their birth was a mistake and that the parents regretted even having them. This could lead to thoughts of cutting, hurting themselves or even suicide.

Our church works with former and some current prisoners and many of these men and women heard these things growing up so it's no wonder they ended up getting into serious trouble when they got older. We should never say these or any other hurtful thing to our child, no matter if they're 9 or 90. Words hurt and even if a child is now grown, a parent's words can cut deeply and hurt badly and some words do irrevocable damage that never heals.

Conclusion

Today's youth do not have to be leaving the church at all if we would only make sure that they have been born again and that must come through the preaching and teaching of the Word, through their involvement in the ministries of the church, by allowing them to serve in certain capacities in real situations, and finally, by mentoring them and having good role models for them to typify. There is hope for the church of tomorrow and that hope is in our youth of today.

Chapter Nine

Ways to Teach Children the Bible

God's Perspective on Children

Children are certainly a blessing and this agrees with what the Bible says about them like in Psalm 127:3-5 "Sons are a heritage from the LORD, children a reward from him. Like arrows in the hands of a warrior are sons born in one's youth. Blessed is the man whose quiver is full of them. They will not be put to shame when they contend with their enemies in the gate." Sons and of course daughters are from the Lord and, I love this, they are "a reward from him." Like the arrows in the hands of a warrior, children are born and like arrows, they are held steady, directed, and aimed but where they land is up to the arrows (or the children). The implication is that we can teach them, direct them, lead them, hold or point them in the right direction but where they land is up to them but hopefully, in God's sovereignty, they will find their purpose. When Esau met his brother Jacob and his family, he said "Who are these with you?" he asked. Jacob answered, "They are the children God has graciously given your servant" (Gen 33:5). Even Jacob got it...children are a gift from our heavenly Father and like a gift, we did nothing to deserve them or earn them...it is only because God is so good that He gives us our beloved children.

Children's Praise is God-ordained

The chief priests were really jealous of Jesus' positon among the people and they were absolutely indignant when they heard the children praising Him in Matthew 21:15b-16 and "shouting in the temple area, "Hosanna to the Son of David," they retorted, "Do you hear what these children are saying?" they asked him. "Yes" replied Jesus, "have you never read, "From the lips of children and infants you have ordained praise?" Jesus knew that the chief priests had probably read this which was from Psalm 8:2 and what made them even madder about this was that Psalm 8 was a praise psalm about God. They understood that this psalm was about the majesty and glory of God and they hated the idea of this psalm being used for praising Jesus but it was completely appropriate being Jesus is God.

Children are generally honest and some of their praises about God are the most sincere and genuine that you'll ever hear. Maybe that's part of the reason that Jesus said that those who are like children will be entering the kingdom of God.

Being Child-like

As I touched on in the earlier paragraph, Jesus "called a little child and had him stand among them. And he said: "I tell you the truth, unless you change and become like little children, you will never enter the kingdom of heaven. Therefore, whoever humbles himself like this child is the greatest in the kingdom of heaven. "And whoever welcomes a little child like this in my name welcomes me. But if anyone causes one of these little ones who believe in me to sin, it would be better for him to have a large millstone hung around his neck and to be drowned in the depths of the sea" (Matt 18:2-6).

Jesus loves children and the fact that we are told to be like children means that we should be teachable, humble, and genuinely honest but being child-like is not the same thing as childish. In fact Jesus said "whoever humbles himself like this child is the greatest in the kingdom of heaven." Since we know that God resists or opposes the proud He will give grace only to the humble (James 4:6). The greatest are not the proud, not the arrogant, not the mighty or the strong…but the humble. This runs contrary to the ways of the world. Also, Jesus gives a very serious warning to anyone who causes these little ones to stumble. The image of a giant millstone being hung around the neck and then cast into the sea is a fierce symbol of God's judgment.

Receiving the Kingdom like a Child

Mark mentions something similar to Matthew 18 when he writes "People were bringing little children to Jesus to have him touch them, but the disciples rebuked them. When Jesus saw this, He was indignant. He said to them, "Let the little children come to me, and do not hinder them, for the kingdom of God belongs to such as these. I tell you the truth, anyone who will not receive the kingdom of God like a little child will never enter it." And he took the children in his arms, put his hands on them and blessed them." This closely resembles the verses in Matthew but there is an important difference as Jesus says that we must receive the kingdom like a child...again, in humility and meekness, otherwise they "will never enter it." The disciples tried to keep the children away from Jesus but He rebuked them and loved them to be near Him, touching them tenderly.

Children are Teachable

The duty of every parent or caregiver, and I would add grandparents too, is to teach their children because God commands parents to do so and will hold them responsible for any negligence in this area. We see this in the Old and the New Testament. Deuteronomy 11:19 gives us an imperative command, "Teach them to your children, talking about them when you sit at home and when you walk along the road, when you lie down and when you get up." Instructing children is a 24/7, seven days a week obligation. We are commanded to teach them when they are sitting at home, when they are traveling or walking "along the road," and when they go to bed (when they "lie down") and in the morning ("when you get up"). This verse is written directly to parents so that they have no excuse to neglect such important instructions about the ways of the Lord. Again, children are teachable and that's a quality that's admirable in adults as well.

As we have read, children are teachable and like sponges, they soak up whatever they are exposed to, for good or the bad. Children are gifts sent directly from heaven by our loving Father. We should praise God with the same genuine, heart-felt admiration that children exude for God. We should be humble like children are because no one who is full of pride and does not humble themselves before God will ever enter the kingdom. And finally, we should receive the kingdom of God like a child does, not pretentiously, not presumptuously, and not with any arrogance at all. Jesus warns us to never be the cause of a little one to stumble or fall. It would have been better for that person not to have been born. We must teach our children and our grandchildren the ways of the Lord, and pray for them, and love them as much as possible the way that Jesus loved us. Our love for children must be unconditional, just as Jesus love was for us, dying for us while we were still His enemies and wicked sinners (Rom 5:8, 10). The Bible describes children in the way He desires us to be. Only then is there any hope of entering God's kingdom.

How to Teach a Sunday School Lesson at Church or Home

What format could a person use to teach a Sunday school class? What biblical model can we use to do this? What if your church doesn't have Sunday school? Here is a way not only how you can teach a Sunday school class but how you can teach your children about God at home.

The Essential of Prayer

No Sunday school lesson should ever be taught without first having prayer. This should be the first thing that you do before class begins and the last thing you should do at the end of class. We must acknowledge that we can only know the things of God by the Spirit of God so ask God for the Holy Spirit that He would help you and the students understand what is being taught, what the context is, and what the outcomes should be. Listen to what Paul told the Corinthian church (1 Cor 1:10-14), "these things God has revealed to us through the Spirit. For the Spirit searches everything, even the depths of God. For who knows a person's thoughts except the spirit of that person, which is in him? So also no one comprehends the thoughts of God except the Spirit of God.

Now we have received not the spirit of the world, but the Spirit who is from God, that we might understand the things freely given us by God. And we impart this in words not taught by human wisdom but taught by the Spirit, interpreting spiritual truths to those who are spiritual. The natural person does not accept the things of the Spirit of God, for they are folly to him, and he is not able to understand them because they are spiritually discerned." Jesus said that "the Advocate, the Holy Spirit, whom the Father will send in my name, will teach you all things and will remind you of everything I have said to you" (John 14:26) and that the "anointing (Holy Spirit) teaches you about all things and as that anointing is real, not counterfeit--just as it has taught you, remain in him" (1 John 2:27).

Sunday School or Bible Lessons

Most churches provide Sunday school teachers with teacher copies of the lessons that are associated with the copies that the students will have. The teacher should attempt to use as much of the Scriptures that are in these lessons as time may permit. If a lesson doesn't have many Scriptures, find some that are relevant to the lessons. The real power of teaching is not in the lessons, it is not in the effectiveness of the teacher, and it is not in the attentiveness of the students...it's what Paul wrote in Romans 1:16 "For I am not ashamed of the gospel, for it is the power of God for salvation to everyone who believes, to the Jew first and also to the Greek." There is your power source; the Word of God. All you have to do is unleash it. You take the Word of God, have the Spirit of God apply it, and you have God's effectual power to enable the student to learn. Undoubtedly," the word of the cross is folly to those who are perishing, but to us who are being saved it is the power of God" (1 Cor 1:18).

If you want to empower students with learning, you must use the Word of God above all of the other teachings in the lesson. This includes Bible commentaries or the Sunday school lesson books; their commentaries might be inspiring but they are not inspired by God. God says that "my word…that goes out from my mouth; it shall not return to me empty, but it shall accomplish that which I purpose, and shall succeed in the thing for which I sent it" (Isaiah 55:11). Use of God's Word is the most important part of any Sunday school teaching. If your church did not provide you with Sunday school lesson books, ask for some. If they are unable to provide them due to financial considerations, then the next few sections of this article, hopefully, can give you other resources. Use the Bible as much as you possibly can; it is the greatest source for God's power there is in teaching Sunday school. When you are reading the Scriptures you will use, be sure and take turns and include everyone.

An Historical Approach

When Stephen was brought before the Jewish leaders for preaching the gospel and accused by false witnesses, what did he do? Stephen gave them a history lesson of the nation of Israel and proved that Jesus was indeed the Messiah and that they had murdered Him (Acts 7). This was a type of apologetic approach that many Sunday school teachers already use. There are so many different portions of the Bible than can be incorporated into Sunday school lessons that there is at least one for every specific lesson that a teacher wants to cover. For example, if you are focusing on evangelism, and every believer is commanded to participate in the Great Commission (Matt 28:18-20; Acts 1:8), you can use Stephen's approach or perhaps Paul's approach when he witnessed to the Greeks in Athens on Mar's Hill (at the Areopagus) in Acts 17. Paul even used some of their own Greek philosophers (17:28) to point them to the One, True God. He spoke of a coming day of judgment and about the resurrection (17:31) and it mattered little to Paul that some mocked his teachings because there were others that wanted to hear more about it and wanted him to speak again on these things (17:32).

The story of the fall of mankind in Genesis is a great beginning point about why we are all born into sin (Psalm 51:5) and was the reason why our sins had separated us from a Holy God (Isaiah 59:1-2), that we became enemies of God because of our sins (Rom 5:10) and this was why Jesus came and lived a sinless life and died for us while we were still sinners (Rom 5:8) and for those who have repented and trusted in Him we now have peace with God (Rom 5:1) and the Father now sees us as having the same righteousness that the Son of God has (2 Cor 5:21). A clear presentation of the gospel should be given in every lesson. Unless the teacher knows how to be saved and knows how to present it, they might not make a good teacher and until the students know what the gospel is (Rom 10:9-13) they can never be saved (if they aren't already) and they won't know how to share it with a lost person.

Is it an Adult, Teen, or Children's Class?

A huge factor in determining how to teach is who you teach. That is, are you going to be teaching adults, teens, or children? If you are teaching adults, you will not need many manipulatives. When I taught adults, I occasionally used examples of things in the lesson that was being taught and the same principle applies to teens. Teens love to watch videos and there are many sterling programs that teach youth from many different resources. As for children, you will want to keep them engaged and so having a certain amount of activities is a great way to teach them about the things of God. Many manipulatives can easily be assimilated into object lessons that relate to your lesson. Having snacks, drawing activities, Bible videos, and hand manipulatives can help to create enthusiasm for young learners. It's good if you can have the child bring something that they created in class to take home with them so that they can show their parents what they did and what was taught in the class.

Additional Helpful Ideas

I love the idea of having name badges or stickers where you can read each person's name. It helps the teacher in the event that they don't know everyone by name. It helps those who have just joined the church or the class too. Make sure and allow them to ask questions. It's a good idea to ask your students questions too to make sure that they understand the lesson and ask open ended questions that don't require a simple yes or a no.

A great way to learn about God and the Bible is to teach a class because the teacher should know more about the lesson than those who are being taught. Make sure that everyone is participating. Give everyone a chance to be included. Don't allow only one or two people to dominate and so ask others "What do you think?" Make sure you have a lesson plan made out as far in advance as possible in the event that you cannot teach the class and a substitute can take your class over if they need to. Things come up. People get sick, others take vacations, still others have unplanned things come up. Make sure and meet with your substitute in advance and have them be familiar with your lessons. Many churches that supply Sunday school books have more than one teacher's book so allow anyone who substitutes for you to have a copy of the lesson book. By all means, get an attendance record started and include the names, ages (if teens or children), and the dates that they attend or are absent.

I taught Sunday school for many years and thoroughly enjoyed it. There are fewer things that are more rewarding than having someone express the desire to be saved. It's very possible that someone in your class is not saved so always open with prayer and close with prayer but always present what the gospel so that everyone can understand what it means to repent, confess their sins, and to put their trust in Christ. Know how to present the gospel like Jesus did. Know what to say to a person who expresses the desire to be saved. Know enough of the important Scriptures that you can turn to when you want to show someone from the Bible how they can be saved (e.g. Rom 10:9-13). If you have a suggestion, please write it down in the comments section below because this article is not a comprehensive article about how to teach Sunday school. I would appreciate learning from you and I am certain others would too.

6 Bible Study Topics for Teens

Are there certain topics that Teenagers can study that apply specifically to them? Yes there are. Explore topics for teens that you might not have thought of.

Teens Who God Used

Teenagers are frequently mentioned in the Bible. These young men and women were used by God in powerful ways. There is Mary, the mother of Jesus, Daniel the young man later turned prophet, the young shepherd boy who would rise to prominence as Israel's greatest king and many others who courageously changed the world for the better. Names like John Mark who wrote the Gospel of Mark with Peter's perspective and Timothy, the young pastor mentored by the Apostle Paul. Teenagers should be able to identify with these young men and women because today, Christian teenagers are still changing the world and helping to transform it as they too can the world upside down (or really, right side up).

Mary, Mother of Jesus

Mary was probably only a girl of 12 or 13 so she qualifies as one of the greatest Bible study topics for teenagers. Look at her response to God's Word by means of an angel of God in Luke 1:26-38: "In the sixth month the angel Gabriel was sent from God to a city of Galilee named Nazareth, to a virgin betrothed to a man whose name was Joseph, of the house of David. And the virgin's name was Mary. And he came to her and said, "Greetings, O favored one, the Lord is with you!" But she was greatly troubled at the saying, and tried to discern what sort of greeting this might be. And the angel said to her, "Do not be afraid, Mary, for you have found favor with God. And behold, you will conceive in your womb and bear a son, and you shall call his name Jesus. He will be great and will be called the Son of the Most High. And the Lord God will give to him the throne of his father David, and he will reign over the house of Jacob forever, and of his kingdom there will be no end." And Mary said to the angel, "How will this be, since I am a virgin?" And the angel answered her, "The Holy Spirit will come upon you, and the power of the Most High will overshadow you; therefore the child to be born will be called holy—the Son of God. And behold, your relative Elizabeth in her old age has also conceived a son, and this is the sixth month with her who was called barren. For nothing will be impossible with God." And Mary said, "Behold, I am the servant of the Lord; let it be to me according to your word." And the angel departed from her."

The angel said that Mary was favored by God. She was certainly chaste as she was still a virgin and what was Mary's response to such an unbelievable call? She said what many teens can say and are saying to God when He speaks to them through His written Word, the Bible, "Behold, I am the servant of the Lord; let it be to me according to your word." God is looking for such godly teens like her today as it says in 2 Chronicles 16:9a "the eyes of the Lord run to and fro throughout the whole earth, to give strong support to those whose heart is blameless toward him." Is that you?

The Teen Daniels Example

We read next about Daniel, who was just a young man when he ran into a test and refused to eat what God had forbid the Jews to eat, ignoring the king's edict, and putting his own life at risk. Read what Daniel did when faced with persecution from a pagan king in Daniel 1:6-16: "Daniel resolved that he would not defile himself with the king's food, or with the wine that he drank. Therefore he asked the chief of the eunuchs to allow him not to defile himself. And God gave Daniel favor and compassion in the sight of the chief of the eunuchs, and the chief of the eunuchs said to Daniel, "I fear my lord the king, who assigned your food and your drink; for why should he see that you were in worse condition than the youths who are of your own age? So you would endanger my head with the king." Then Daniel said to the steward whom the chief of the eunuchs had assigned over Daniel, Hananiah, Mishael, and Azariah, "Test your servants for ten days; let us be given vegetables to eat and water to drink. Then let our appearance and the appearance of the youths who eat the king's food be observed by you, and deal with your servants according to what you see." So he listened to them in this matter, and tested them for ten days. At the end of ten days it was seen that they were better in appearance and fatter in flesh than all the youths who ate the king's food. So the steward took away their food and the wine they were to drink, and gave them vegetables."

Daniel refused to defile himself with unclean foods. It may have been because "And God gave Daniel favor and compassion in the sight of the chief of the eunuchs." The chief of the eunuchs feared for Daniel's life if he didn't eat what the king had assigned or ordered for them to eat. The eunuch feared for his own head too but Daniel convinced "the steward whom the chief of the eunuchs had assigned over Daniel, Hananiah, Mishael, and Azariah." They allowed Daniel to challenge them to who would be "better in appearance and fatter in the flesh (or healthier) than all the youths who ate the king's food." After the test of ten days were up, clearly Daniel and the other three young men were in much better shape and health by not taking the king's diet. They refused to eat the king's food and drink his wine at risk to their own life. Daniel may not have even been of age in our society today, but he showed restraint in not drinking wine and gorging on exorbitant food, and he showed that when we obey God, God is pleased and God blesses those who obey Him. Daniel chose to do the right thing, even if it meant disobeying a king who held his life in his hands.

David, from Shepherd to King

David was called by God a man after His own heart. Why so? It was because David was humble in nature and trusted in God and strived to be obedient to Him. David was a teen when he faced Goliath, the greatest and biggest warrior of the ancient world. Based upon a human comparison, David had no chance of taking on such a giant of a man. Goliath was fully armored and completely equipped. David had only a slingshot and five stones. When David heard Goliath slandering God and His chosen people, he was livid. How did he react when he heard God's name being insulted? It is recorded in 1 Samuel 17: 31-37: "When the words that David spoke were heard, they repeated them before Saul, and he sent for him. And David said to Saul, "Let no man's heart fail because of him. Your servant will go and fight with this Philistine." And Saul said to David, "You are not able to go against this Philistine to fight with him, for you are but a youth, and he has been a man of war from his youth." But David said to Saul, "Your servant used to keep sheep for his father. And when there came a lion, or a bear, and took a lamb from the flock, I went after him and struck him and delivered it out of his mouth. And if he arose against me, I caught him by his beard and struck him and killed him. Your servant has struck down both lions and bears, and this uncircumcised Philistine shall be like one of them, for he has defied the armies of the living God." And David said, "The Lord who delivered me from the paw of the lion and from the paw of the bear will deliver me from the hand of this Philistine." And Saul said to David, "Go, and the Lord be with you!"

David had no fear for he feared God above man. Is that you? When you face your own giants, will you trust in the Lord and obey Him at all costs? David must have trusted God as he said that God will "deliver me from the hand of this Philistine." David's trust of the Lord and his fierce determination to protect the sanctified name of God made him a teen hero and the perfect candidate for the next king of Israel and the best king in Israel's history. My dear teen friend, do you uphold the holiness of God's name in your world? Would you also be offended when someone blasphemes God's name? Trust in God and fight for what is right and if you obey Him, He will deliver you through the many trials and tests in this world, even if they are gigantic in size.

Bad Company Corrupts Good People

Let's look at three other Bible studies topics that teens can use. In 1 Corinthians 14:33-34 Paul writes "Let us eat and drink, for tomorrow we die." Do not be deceived: "Bad company ruins good morals." Wake up from your drunken stupor, as is right, and do not go on sinning. For some have no knowledge of God. I say this to your shame." The lesson here is that a person can become like those that they run with. My wife and I are Christians. She influences me positively and I hope I do her. We also influence our children, hopefully for the better. The more they are with us as they've grown up, the more our influence has impacted the way they are. If we were horrible parents then they might turn out horribly. The point is that if you run with those whose feet are swift to run to evil, you will find yourself in their shoes more and more often and getting into more trouble. Truly, bad company corrupts good people.

To Find a Friend, Be a friend.

You are going to need to surround yourself with godly friends. There is so much peer pressure these days to run with the crowd. If you have godly young men and women as friends, you are more likely to have a positive peer pressure (to do the right thing) than a negative peer pressure (pressuring you to sin). Proverbs 17:17 says "A friend loves at all times, and a brother is born for adversity." A friend loves you through the good times and the bad. They can help support you and encourage you through times of adversity. There are no lone ranger Christians in the New Testament churches. If you want a godly friend then be a godly friend. Teens need godly teens because two are better than one, especially if they are believers who believe and act more like you.

Jesus is your friend no matter what age you are. The teens in the Bible I mentioned are ones that even adults should emulate. Find a godly teen that you can become best of friends with and then maybe they will say this about you, "These [young] men [and women] who have turned the world upside down have come here also" (Acts 17:6b).

5 Bible Stories to Teach To Young Children

What five Bible stories would be good to teach young children? What specifically can we impart to them that they can carry with them for the rest of their lives?

The Prodigal Son

The Parable of the Prodigal Son is one of the tenderest stories in the Bible. The story is told in Luke 15:11-32 and has the younger son coming to his father and asking for his inheritance ahead of time. This is essentially telling his father "I wish you were dead. Give me my inheritance now." The father gives him what he asks for and then the son leaves and spends all of it on sinful activities. When the boy runs out of money he ends up working for a pig farmer and is so hungry that he ends up desiring the slop that he feeds the pigs with. Finally, when he hits rock bottom and realizes that even his father's hired hands (servants) have it better than he does, he returns to his father, ready to ask for his forgiveness. The lesson here is that since the prodigal's father was looking down the road for his son's return and then ran out to greet him, how much more so can parents love their children unconditionally and always be willing to forgive them? Parental love should be like that of the prodigal son's father.

Parents should be eager to see their children return and then run to greet them and be swift in forgiving them. Children who see this story reflected in their parent's love for them stand a better chance at returning from the "pig pen" of their lives with no fear of condemnation. We should give them what they don't deserve because God loved us while we were still His enemies and still yet sinning (Rom 5:8, 11).

David and Goliath

The story of David versus Goliath in 1 Samuel 17 reminds children that we all face giants in our lives from time to time but faith or trust in God can help us not to be overwhelmed for Paul wrote that if God is for us, who in this world could ever be against us (Rom 8:31)? Can this story help when our children face the inevitable bullies in school? I believe it can.

The main lesson in this story is that it is actually God who delivered Goliath into David's hand and not David. David confidently said "The Lord, who delivered me from the paw of the lion and from the paw of the bear, He will deliver me from the hand of this Philistine" (1 Sam 17:37). When David finally faced Goliath, listen to his confidence, not in himself, but in God: "David said to the Philistine, "You come to me with a sword, with a spear, and with a javelin. But I come to you in the name of the Lord of hosts, the God of the armies of Israel, whom you have defied. This day the Lord will deliver you into my hand, and I will strike you and take your head from you. And this day I will give the carcasses of the camp of the Philistines to the birds of the air and the wild beasts of the earth, that all the earth may know that there is a God in Israel. Then all this assembly shall know that the Lord does not save with sword and spear; for the battle is the Lord's, and He will give you into our hands" (1 Sam 17:45-47).

We need to teach our children that the battles in this life must be fought in God's strength and not in our own and that in time, maybe not that day, God will avenge us and so we must trust Him to repay our enemies (Rom 12:19). It is not our duty to avenge those who wrong us but leave this up to the Just Judge, God, and actually pray for our enemies (Matt 5:44).

Noah's Ark

This story is one of redemption but also includes the wrath of God. God is slow to anger and merciful but in time, God saw "that the wickedness of man was great in the earth, and that every intent of the thoughts of his heart was only evil continually" (Gen 6:5), meaning that wickedness is all that mankind thought about and "that every intent of [their] heart was only evil continually." In other words, all they thought about was sinning and every intentional thought was bent toward evil and when a person reaches that stage, God must move in wrath to judge this unrepentant sinner. Even so, God still allowed Noah to preach so that they could be spared from God's wrath if they repented and put their trust in Him.

Noah probably preached repentance during the many years it took him and his family to build the Ark but God knew that mankind was not interested in repentance and all they thought about was new ways to sin. Since "Noah did according to all that God commanded him" (Gen 6:22) and that Noah alone was "righteous before [Him] in this generation" (Gen 7:1b) God was going to spare his family from the coming flood, which is a picture or image of His judgment upon sin. Something that is easily missed is the language which describes that God was on the ark already as God said "Come into the ark, you and all your household" (Gen 7:1a). If God were outside of the ark He would have said "go into the ark" but if someone is inside their home and they were to ask you to "come in," they wouldn't say "go into the house" but they would say "come into the house" because they were already inside. This language signifies that God was with Noah and his family and it wasn't Noah who closed the ark's door but it was "the LORD [WHO] shut him in" (Gen 7:16c). This also shows that salvation is fully a work of God and not of man.

And God was with Joseph

When Joseph was unfairly sold into slavery by his brothers (Gen 38:1), Joseph didn't wail or complain by saying "Why God?" but he simply understood that God's would work out all things out in time, no matter what his life looked like (Rom 8:28) and time and again the Scriptures said that "The Lord was with Joseph" (Gen 39:2a). Even when Joseph was unfairly thrown into prison, it was still said that "the Lord was with him; and whatever he did, the Lord made it prosper" (Gen 39:23c). It's interesting to note that almost 1/3rd of the Book of Genesis was about Joseph which means that the story of Joseph must have been very important to God. Frequently, when there are many Scriptures given to a subject or topic, it is important to God. For example, God's Law has the longest chapter in the Bible (Psalm 119) showing that God's Law and obedience to it is especially important to God. Similarly, much of Genesis is reserved for the story of Joseph and how we often suffer unfairly but God is still with us even when He is silent.

Prior to Joseph's account, God directly spoke to the Patriarchs but God never directly spoke to Joseph but it was still written, time and again, that "the Lord was with Joseph." A take away from this story would be that children will find out soon enough that life is not fair but that doesn't mean that God isn't with them throughout these unfair trials.

Daniel in the Lion's Den

In Daniel chapter six we see that Daniel was thrown into the lion's den because he would rather obey God and pray to Him than to pray to a pagan king. Daniel may have thought that his life was about to end but this didn't stop him from doing what is right. Even King Darius didn't want Daniel to die and so spent a sleepless night trying to think of a way to save him while not going against his own decree that he had been tricked into writing by Daniel's enemies who were jealous of his position of authority (Dan 6:2-5). When Daniel was helpless he had a God Who was not. God stopped the lion's mouth through an angel of God (Dan 6:22) showing that God is still sovereign over nature, rulers, and all beasts of the earth (Dan 6:23-27). The lesson children could learn here is that no matter what things look like, God is still in control. Nothing gets by Him and He defends the defenseless. Sometimes we will be hated because of our faith or sometimes people will be jealous of us but we must do what is right because "We ought to obey God rather than men" (Acts 5:29).

Conclusion

Every one of us will have to face our giants in this life, we will all be treated unfairly at some point, we'll all be put into positions that look impossible to get out of, and God desires that everyone repents and trusts in Him. God is a God of mercy and desires that all be saved (1 Tim 2:4) but He is also a God of wrath (John 3:36b) and cannot overlook sin (Rom 3:23, 6:23) but while we were still sinners, He died for us (Rom 5:8) so if you repent today and put your trust in Him, you too can be spared (John 3:16-17)...even if you are shut up in a lion's den.

Reasons Creationism Should be Taught in School and Home

Should creationism be taught alongside evolution? Is it fair to give students only one theory to believe? Is it legal to do so in the public schools?

There are No Criticisms of Evolution

There are no criticisms of the theory of evolution in any of the textbooks or course material. Evolution has never been classified as a scientific law and has remained a theory for a century. For one thing, evolution cannot be validated to be true because it cannot be proven through scientific testing. How can evolution ever be established by scientific methods to be shown to be true in an empirical and conclusive way? Can evolution ever be observed in a laboratory? Is evolution something that is repeatable? Is it predictable as to what mankind will look like a million years from now? How can it be falsified? The classic historical structure of having scientific beliefs pass from theory to law is by having something be observed, repeated, to make predictions based upon those observations, and have a repeated outcome and then falsify the results so that it proves it is true.

Evolution is a historically based theory based upon assumptions from what took place millions of years ago. What are missing are the gaps of transitional fossils that establish one specie evolving into another, new specie. When there is yet another claim that a missing link has been found, the question arises, where is the chain in the first place? How can we claim to have found a missing link while there isn't even a chain? Maybe you've seen the images or pictures of man evolving from apes in textbooks. What are missing are transitional fossils between the ape and man so educators have to depend upon images and drawings to try and establish a connection. Why? It's because there are no fossils that they can take pictures of to display as proof.

Scientists have at their disposal, hundreds of millions of fossils and fossil samples, yet not one set of transitional fossils revealing specie evolving into another has ever been found. Despite untold millions of categorized fossils their remains no set that establish a new life form evolving from another. This fact was not lost by Darwin who said that he was troubled by the lack of fossil evidence showing that new species arose from previous ones.

92

Critical Thinking Skills

It seems that public schools value critical thinking skills yet they are cramming an unproven theory down the student's throats and so it appears that they won't even consider other possibilities. These educators are like dictators who essentially spout "It's my way or the highway." Since educational leadership want students to think "outside the box" in the other disciplines, why aren't they allowed to do so regarding the theory of evolution. They say that they want the students to use their minds to solve problems, analyze issues, to critique thesis's, but how can a student do this if they are taught that the theory of evolution has no alternatives. There are no other options, no other possibilities. They are taught that there are no exceptions to the theory of evolution.

The educational textbooks are silent on the problematic areas of evolution. For example, evolution does not address the question of where did the universe come from. How did the universe come into existence? How did life arise since we know for a fact that life cannot arise spontaneously? The theory of evolution is like coming into a movie that is half way through to the end. What happened before life got here? How was non-living, inorganic matter able to come to life? The theory of evolution only deals with the fact that life had already existed and that life forms evolve into new species.

It seems to me that they are leaving out some crucial components. It doesn't address the cause of these effects, how a universe from a singular point began or what forces were involved and necessary to have that first spark of life occur. What about the Cambrian Explosion, a layer where almost every single life form is found in fossil form with few ancestral fossils before it or no new life fossil life forms above it? This sounds more like a philosophy than it does a science. Children should be at least exposed to or taught other views and be allowed to make their own decisions based upon the information or the lack of information that they have.

Give Parents What They Want

A 1991 Gallop Poll (Nov 28th, 1991), which was the last time a comprehensive polling results on a national scale was undertaken, indicated that 47% of Americans believe in creation over evolution and 40% believe that God used evolution as a process of creating life. A few had no opinion and so that left only 9% of Americans who believe that God was not involved and that only naturalistic means were the cause of the origin of life. Since almost 9 out of every 10 Americans believe that God was involved in creation and just under half of those believed that the origin of life was not naturalistically caused, why do almost 100% of college professors and staff teach that evolution is the only option possible? These professors and the colleges seem to be in the minority, yet they do not tolerate differences of opinion or belief, even though the theory of evolution has never been comprehensively established as a fact. Why not let people choose what they want their children to learn? Don't these professors and colleges work for the students who pay their salaries or the parents who educate their children? Why is there no tolerance for those who differ in opinions and hold to a different belief than an unproven, untested theory? Good question. Children should be taught that evolution is only a theory and to see that a theory is not the same as a scientific law like Newton's Three Laws of Motion.

Freedom of Speech

I believe that students should have the option of stating their own beliefs and base them upon what findings they gain in their education. Former President George Bush once said that "Both sides ought to be properly taught so people can understand what the debate is about. Part of education is to expose people to different schools of thought [and] people ought to be exposed to different ideas." Academic freedom is what brought the theory of evolution to the classrooms in the first place and so what is wrong with the idea of allowing others to provide their views on how life came into being and if it did evolve or didn't evolve. Shouldn't we let them freely express what they believe and provide the reasons for why they believe what they do believe? Good science has always allowed for controversy in the classroom and so educators should allow for rational scientific discussion and criticisms of the theory of evolution. By the way, educators should not state that evidence for Darwinian evolution is overwhelming and indisputable.

Evolution is Bad Science

Mankind used to believe that the earth was flat and that if a ship sailed too far it would end up falling off the edge of the earth. That is because we believed only with our eyes. The theory of evolution is much like this in that a theory or belief is taught as scientific fact because of what they perceive even though nothing could be further from the truth. Teaching evolution as fact is just plain bad science. Evolution is closer to a philosophy than it is a science. One example is that mutations are a good thing.

I heard about a dairy farmer who had a dairy cow that gave birth to a calf with two heads. That is a mutation. The problem was that the calf died since it was sending different signals to its digestive system and survived for only a few days. If you had asked the dairy farmer if that mutation was an advantage, he would have said no because the calf died. I have never seen or heard of a mutation where it helped the specie propagate or survive and become a better organism.

If you asked biologists if mutations are a good thing, they might give you a funny look because mutations are basically a change that takes place in the nucleotide sequence within the genome of an organism. These mutations are the result of DNA or DNA genomes that were unrepaired and will lead to errors in the replication process of additional cells. Even so, evolutionists claim that mutations are how life forms eventually evolve into a new life form. Evolution requires positive mutations, which are so rare that scientists have problems finding them in nature. What they do find are mutations that are extremely harmful and sometimes fatal to the organism. In order for evolution to work it needs an increase in information by means of positive mutations. The only problem is they can't find where this occurs by natural means.

Another good example of bad science in the theory of evolution is that they keep claiming to find missing links and that these links are the "smoking gun" of evidence in the fossil layer. The only roaring evidence is the roaring silence in the fossil record. This was exactly the reason that Darwin had great doubts in his theory because he couldn't find any transitional fossils showing evidence that specie evolved into other life forms.

How do they explain the Cambrian explosion or the Cambrian rock, where there are exceedingly few fossils that come before the Cambrian layers? There are primarily only three such fossils and they lay adjacent to the Cambrian layer, as close in fact as to almost appear in that layer. One example is the Cloudina and Namacalathus mineral tubular fossils. Despite the claim that they are millions of years old they remain virtually unchanged today from when they first appeared! Then there are the Mollusc-like Kimberella and its trace fossils (also unchanged as of today) and then the Mollusc-like Kimberella and its trace fossils. Needless to say, these too have not changed at all. Why haven't they evolved or changed by increased information as a result of "positive mutations?" Incidentally, the Cloudina are the oldest known evidence in the fossil record of the calcified skeletal formation in metazoans, a prominent feature in animals appearing in the Early Cambrian and not before. There is also good fossil evidence that exists for the appearance of gastropods, cephalopods and bivalves which are classified as Mollusc-like Kimberella and its trace fossils, which by the way, are also found in the Cambrian period.

Recently, the fossil record of the earliest animals from the Ediacaran to the Cambrian was made but the dating and interpretation of these remain controversial. As Wikipedia has stated, "The long-running puzzlement about the appearance of the Cambrian fauna, seemingly abruptly and from nowhere, centers on three key points: whether there really was a mass diversification of complex organisms over a relatively short period of time during the early Cambrian; what might have caused such rapid change; and what it would imply about the origin and evolution of animals. Interpretation is difficult due to a limited supply of evidence, based mainly on an incomplete fossil record and chemical signatures remaining in Cambrian rocks." So, it is not only up to interpretation but this interpretation is difficult "due to a limited supply of evidence" and it is "based mainly on incomplete fossil records and chemical signatures remaining in Cambrian rocks." The words "interpretation" and the fact that there is a "limited supply of evidence...due to an incomplete fossil record" sound highly speculative and subjective at best.

Conclusion

Part of the reason that creationism or at least, intelligent design should be allowed to be discussed in the classroom is because evolution presents a world view without God and that there is only "survival of the fittest" and that there is no real purpose for mankind other than "eat, drink, and be merry for tomorrow we die." The theory of evolution portrays mankind as only a collection of molecules as a result of blind, accidental chance with the only reason we were born was to survive.

Chapter Ten

The Importance of Parents

The Prodigal Children

What would you say to your prodigal children or grandchildren?

Isaiah 43:5-6 "Fear not, for I am with you; I will bring your offspring from the east, and from the west. I will gather you, Do not withhold; bring my sons from afar and my daughters from the end of the earth."

Never Give Up

You may not even be able to say anything to you prodigals right now. Perhaps your prodigal son or daughter or grandchildren won't even talk to you anymore. Perhaps it's because they are under conviction that the life they are living is wrong. Maybe you've pressured them too much but whatever their state, never give up on them and continually pray for them. I realize that Isaiah 43 is about Israel returning to God but surely this could be said about God's desire that our prodigals would return to Him too. In the first place, it is God Who does the saving (Acts 2:47) but we can at least never faint or never waver in our prayers for them (Luke 18:1) because love never, ever fails (1 Cor 13:8).

Tell them you Love Them

Even if all you can tell them is that you love them, don't fail to tell them that just because they haven't returned to you or to the Lord. God is patient and long-suffering and He doesn't want any of them to perish (2 Pet 3:9). The word used for long-suffering means to be extraordinarily patient...almost supernaturally patient and since that is what God is toward us, we must be toward our prodigals. The Greek word used for the word long-suffering, some translations say patient, is "makrothymeō" and it means "to be of a long spirit, to not lose heart, to persevere patiently and bravely" so that is what the prodigal parents and grandparents must do. Never let them see you lose your patience over there being a prodigal because that might make them more resistant to coming back to you. The more loving and patient you remain, the easier it will be for them if they decide to come back and the last thing we want to do is to make it harder for them to come back to us.

Keep the Lines Open

Just imagine your prodigals as being on the other end of a phone line and if you say the wrong thing in anger or frustration, they might just hang up. By all means, keep that line of communication open because God might send them His Spirt to convict them of where they are at (Ezk 11:19-20). You can still send those Christmas cards, birthday cards, and even a greeting card for no particular occasion. Let them hit rock bottom if that's what it takes. The last thing you might want to do is to just keep sending them money because you might be getting between the rock (the bottom) and the hammer (God's working in their lives). If you keep sending them money, you might just be enabling them to continue to stay away.

A Closing Prayer for Prodigals

Great God in heaven, we all at one time, were prodigals. I myself ran from You oh God for so many years but I know according to the Bible that you sent the hounds of heaven in pursuing me with a holy, passionate love that never gave up on me. Thank You Lord for never giving up on me when others would have and should have long ago and I pray these things in Jesus' precious name, amen.

The Importance of Parents

Charles Spurgeon, the Prince of Preachers, said "If we never have headaches through rebuking our children, we shall have plenty of heartaches when they grow up."

Reaping and Sowing

We all know that we always reap what we sow but we reap much later than we sow, so the labor we put into the harvest today will not produce a crop until much later. The greater the labor, the greater the harvest so the same principle applies with children; the more we invest in them, the more we and they will benefit later. What Charles Spurgeon was basically saying was that today's headaches produce fewer heartaches later in life but the fewer the headaches today, the more heartaches we'll have later in life when they get older and are grown. Do the hard work today and reap the joy later but slothfulness in disciplining children today will lead to society doing it for them when they're older...but with far more serious consequences.

Love, Hate, and Apathy

The opposite of love is not hate, it is apathy or indifference. If a child is left to themselves, then they'll see that as hate because the child will see that they really didn't care. The Bible equates no discipline with hating the child as we read in Proverbs 13:24 "Whoever spares the rod hates their children, but the one who loves their children is careful to discipline them." Love and discipline are joined at the hip. You can't show love without discipline and if there is no love, there is usually little or no discipline. When my son was very young, I disciplined him for playing near the street because I loved him and didn't want him to get hurt or killed. If I left him alone, then I'd be showing him that I really hate him in the sense that I don't care what happens to him. Proverbs 29:16 says "The rod and reproof give wisdom, but a child left to himself brings shame to his mother." The "rod" doesn't refer to beating them with one but the rod represents discipline but a child left to themselves will bring shame to the parents.

Turning the Hearts, Saving the Land

In Malachi 4:6 he writes something very interesting "And he will turn the hearts of fathers to their children and the hearts of the children to their fathers, lest I come and strike the land with a decree of utter destruction." Malachi associates turning the hearts of their children to their fathers but what must come first? Just as it says in the order of the sentence; the hearts of the fathers must first be turned to their children or their children's hearts will never be turned to their fathers. What happens if the father's hearts don't turn to their children? The land will be destroyed. Why? Because families are the foundation of any nation and when fathers don't turn to their children's hearts, the children grow up with hearts of stone. These children bear children with the same tendencies and before you know it, the land has no heart for God and it is destroyed.

5 Important Bible Verses for Mothers to Learn

What are some of the most important Bible verses relating to mothers in the Bible? What can they tell us about how to be a godly mother and how we should value our own mother and honor her?

The Stored Treasure in a Mother's Heart

Luke 2:51 "And he went down with them and came to Nazareth and was submissive to them. And his mother treasured up all these things in her heart."

This happened just after Jesus was missing from the traveling party that left Jerusalem after the feast and Jesus' parents discovered that he was not with them and so returned to find Him and upon finding Him in the temple Jesus was "submissive to them" and returned to Nazareth with His family. Jesus had told them why He was still in the Temple and asked His parents, "Why were you looking for me? Did you not know that I must be about my Father's business?" This is what Mary treasured up in her heart but not this alone, she remembered the whole thing and why it was said that "his mother treasured up all these things in her heart." Mothers have a way of storing up these treasures and placing them in the strong box of their hearts. Mothers have better memories than scrap books and can treasure or store up these many precious memories of their children for eternity. Are there any places that have more treasure stored in them than in a mother's heart?

Honoring Your Mother

Ephesians 6:2-3 "Honor your father and mother" (this is the first commandment with a promise), "that it may go well with you and that you may live long in the land."

This is the first commandment with a promise and this promise is that if you honor your father and your mother, you will live long on the earth. Paul is citing Exodus 20:12 where God told Israel, and by extension He tells believers today, that the days of your life can be extended if you honor your parents. This is the first commandment given to mankind as the first four relate to God (mankind's relationship to God and are vertical) but the very first of the next six commandments (are horizontal, mankind dealing with one another) given to mankind is to honor their parents because by honoring them, you are actually honoring God.

A mother should be honored because she has given birth to you; she has nursed you in the selfless, sacrifice of the many early morning feedings and changings. She has nurtured you and fed you and is more responsible for you growing up than the father is. Even though a father may provide for the family, it is the mothers who are the tenderhearted caregivers and do more for their children than anyone else will perhaps ever do in a lifetime. A mother will never give up on her children even when everyone else does. She loves her children unconditionally, even a son who sits on death row. There are fewer things more precious than a mother's love and it has been said that children can actually die from a lack of love...not a problem when a mother is around.

A Mother Never Forgets

Isaiah 49:15 "Can a woman forget her nursing child, that she should have no compassion on the son of her womb? Even these may forget, yet I will not forget you."

You might have forgotten that skinned knee that sent you home crying for your mother. It's interesting that when children get hurt they don't run crying to their father, they usually turn to their mother. She is there to tenderly wipe away ever tear and kiss ever "boo boo." How can she ever forget that precious bundle that she carried so safely in her womb? Isaiah asks the rhetorical question: Can a woman forget her nursing child or have no compassion for the son or daughter she carried for nine months? Of course she can't. Others may forget but a mother never does.

Forever a Mother

Proverbs 23:22 "Listen to your father who gave you life, and do not despise your mother when she is old."

Sadly, mothers are often despised when they get older but a mother is always going to be a mother no matter what age the child is. A mother's love has no expiration date and to her children, even in their old age, they are still and always will be her babies. How quickly we forget once we are out of the home. As I have visited nursing homes, I have seen the aching loneness and crushing emptiness as mothers talked so lovingly about their children...children who cannot seem to find the time to visit them. The tears that she used to wipe away are left alone to run down her sweet cheeks and sometimes live out a life of quiet desperation because most mothers will outlive their children's fathers and they are the ones usually left alone. They often feel neglected and despised and unwanted even though the Bible teaches that we should honor or mothers even "when [they are] old." This is a real heartbreaker and you know God is not pleased because abandoning mothers in their old age breaks the commandment to honor them. The Fourth Commandment also does not expire with time.

Honoring Your Mother is Fearing God

Proverbs 19:26 "He who does violence to his father and chases away his mother is a son who brings shame and reproach."

I once did a home visit and this young man lived with his mom but she was actually afraid of him. I wanted to remember the verse that said "Every one of you shall revere his mother and his father." Some translations say, and I like it better, that "you shall ever man fear every man his mother, and his father." This fear or reverence is often gone when the child gets older but when a child shows his or her mother no respect and they rule the home by fear, they are actually heaping up the anger of God day by day (Prov 19:26) and more so today because this seems to be "a generation [that] curses their father, and does not bless their mother" (Prov 30:11). Someday they will utterly regret this. Here was a setting where the grown son was living in his mother's house yet he ruled the home and talked despairingly to his mother. How sad for her. This young man's life is not going to be as long on this earth as it could have been had he honored, respected, and revered his mother but instead he ordered her around, took advantage of her generosity and even cussed at her (Eph 6:2-3; Ex 21:17).

If you have or had a godly mother, you should thank God for her because a godly, Christian mother is the best source for growing up as a godly man or woman. Perhaps Paul didn't have a godly mother like Timothy did and why he was moved to tears as he thought of this in addressing Timothy, "As I remember your tears, I long to see you, that I may be filled with joy. I am reminded of your sincere faith, a faith that dwelt first in your grandmother Lois and your mother Eunice and now, I am sure, dwells in you as well" (2 Tim 1:4-5). The source or root of Timothy's faith was his mother and his grandmother.

I strongly urge you to always remember your mother, even when she becomes a grandmother for honoring your mother is pleasing to God for God has sovereignly placed her there in your life and nothing or no one can replace the love of a mother because deep is the treasure trove in her heart, she never forgets, and there will not be a day when she is not your mother. You should call her, write or visit her and tell her that you thank God for her.

Children are the next generation so what are you teaching them?

Deuteronomy 4:9 "Only take care, and keep your soul diligently, lest you forget the things that your eyes have seen, and lest they depart from your heart all the days of your life. Make them known to your children and your children's children."

The Command to Teach Them

God commands parents and really grandparents too, to teach their children and their grandchildren. It's not an option. God will hold parents accountable for what they teach and what they don't teach their children. God commanded Israel to gather together, including the children, so that they could hear His words that they should learn to fear Him (Duet 4:10a) but it was also for the purpose of having their children learn about God (Duet 4:10b). This teaching was to be for them, for their children and for their children's children (Duet 4:9) or their grandchildren. God taught His statutes and commands so that it would go well for the nation but also for their children that would come after them so that they might live a long life (Duet 4:40). The very first commandment, the 5th

Commandment, that given to the people in relating to one another was for children to honor their father and their mother because the foundation of any society is the family and this is the only commandment with a promise for the children to live a long life (Eph 6:2).

Teaching Day and Night, Here and There

God once again instructs parents to teach their children when they sit down with you at home, when they are traveling with you, when they go to bed at night, and when they get up in the morning (Duet 6:7; 11:19) but the Word of God should be made visible to them as well in the home (Duet 11:20) and if they did this, once again God promised them a long life and that they would spread out throughout the entire land (Duet 11:21). The Bible mentions the word "children" almost 460 times and if you include the words "sons and daughter" it's close to 1000 times, signifying just how important teaching our children is to Him. Negligent parents are sinning parents as far as God is concerned. We know that if children are left to themselves, they'll bring heartache and shame to their parents (Prov 29:15) and parental neglect includes a lack of discipline (Prov 13:24).

Teaching by Example

Sometimes children learn more from watching parents than from anything that they might say. For example, if someone calls your home and you tell the children that you're not at home, they'll learn to lie when they are placed in situations that they don't like. If we drive over the speed limit consistently, then our children will learn that it's okay to break the law because their parents did it. And if they talk behind someone's back, they'll learn that there's nothing wrong with gossiping about someone. What you do will not only be perceived as normal but as acceptable, no matter what you teach them. They will more likely do what you do than do what you say. They are watching you. Teach them and lead them by example.

That's perhaps the greatest teaching of all that they will ever receive.

Provoked to Anger

It is so easy for parents to provoke their children to anger and then have them grow discouraged (Col 3:21) but parents should bring up their children using discipline and instructing them in the ways of God but doing so out of love (Eph 6:4). If you are a grandparent, you are also told to teach them what you have learned from God as well (Duet 4:9). God the Father disciplines us since He corrects every one of His children (Heb 12:6) but He does it in love. We must model discipline in our own lives and in our children's lives for their own best interests, even when it goes against the grain of society. Just like a parent disciplines the children he or she loves, so too does God discipline us, His own children (Duet 8:5) and those who the Lord disciplines are actually blessed (Psalm 94:12). If we avoid disciplining children then it shows we really don't love them (Prov 13:24) so the way God looks at it is that love equals discipline and discipline equals love. I've talked to many prisoners who wished that their parents would have disciplined them more.

Love Them Like Jesus Does

Jesus loves children and actually loves them more than we do so He never wants us to hinder the children when they need to come to us since Jesus always received children and bid them to always come to Him (Luke 18:15-17). Parents can learn from children because they are humble, they are teachable and little ones with this type of nature will be the ones who will inherit the kingdom of heaven (Matt 19:14). When my youngest daughter asked me once to have a "tea party" with her, I found time; when she asked me to tickle her, I did and once she even asked me to wear a tutu (although I'd deny it in public) but I did, so I found time for her when she wanted her daddy. I wanted to receive her when she came to me just as Jesus received the children and bid them to come to Him.

The most important thing a father can do for his children is to love their mother.   Topics: Fathers, Mothers, Parents   Henry Ward Beecher

3 Reasons Fathers Must Love Their Children's Mother

The Model

Children are given the commandment to honor their father and their mother (Ex 20:12) but that would much harder to do for children if their father doesn't love their mother. How could they honor someone who isn't being loving to their own mother? Children take the treatment of their mother very personally and why shouldn't they. Imagine trying to like someone who treats your mother in a bad way. How hard would it be for you to love that person? Wouldn't it make you mad if someone treated your own mother with contempt?   That's why fathers must love their children's mother because it's going to be hard for them to honor their father if he does not love their own mother.

The Example

Paul instructed Titus to "Show yourself in all respects to be a model of good works, and in your teaching show integrity, dignity, and sound speech that cannot be condemned, so that an opponent may be put to shame, having nothing evil to say about us" (Titus 2:7-8). Paul also wrote to Timothy to "set an example for the believers in speech, in conduct, in love, in faith and in purity" (1 Tim 4:12). If Paul wanted Timothy and Titus to set good examples then examples must be important on how big of an impression they leave on others. So too is the example of how a father loves the mother of his children. They will see this modeled and more likely try to be the same way to their own children when they have them. Jesus "Christ also suffered for you, leaving you an example, so that you might follow in his steps" (1 Pet 2:21) once again showing just how important being an example is.

The Pattern

Children love to imitate people and sometimes things. When my son was very young, he loved imitating an airplane or a dog. They mimic those things they see and hear and so in the same way, they will pattern their lives after the pattern left by their parents. Like father, like son, and like daughter like mother is very true so fathers must be careful in how they talk to their children's mother, how they treat her, how they talk about her when she's not there, and how they show their love by affection and by serving her. The pattern of a child's life is set very early in life and it's ten times more difficult to unlearn something than it is to learn it the first place, so fathers, you have a great responsibility to your children because the most important thing a father can do for his children is to love their mother.

There is such a huge impact on what children see and hear and so fathers have a great responsibility to be loving their children, nurturing them, training them but also in how they treat their children's mother because your words will be drowned out by your actions and they can't hear what you're saying because what you're doing is all they see.

4 Ways to Grow Closer To Your Children

Here are five ways you can grow closer to your children. Can you think of some other ways?

Play with Them

I remember when my daughter was young, I was invited to a "tea party" with her and even though the tea was invisible, I still acted like I drank it. I even wore a tutu with her once (although I will deny it publically) and she got a real hoot out of that. I was willing to play with her and jump into her imaginary world. That's okay. It drew us closer together and those memories still linger today and will forever. Perhaps if she has her own daughter someday, it'll bring back some precious memories. When my son was younger we went to the park and got in the swings next to each other, crashing into one another (boys are so different!) and he laughed so hard I thought he'd fall out of his swing. He has his own children today but still remembers playing "crash dummies" with me in the park. These things drew me closer together with my son and daughter and the memories will never fade away.

Listening and Asking

I think that we should always listen to our children and put down the newspaper or turn the TV off or get off the Internet if our children are talking to us. I need to give them my full attention and eye contact as a sign of respect showing them I value that what they have to say is important. I also like to ask them open-ended questions that don't require a "yes" or a "no" so I can find out how their day went, what happened or is there something on their mind. For example instead of "How was your day" they would say "fine" I would rather ask them, "What happened today at school?"

Hugs and Kisses

I know teens might squirm at this but inwardly, they crave your attention just as a younger child does. I read studies about a nursery in Romania during World War Two that said some of the orphaned children in the nursery were dying even though they had adequate food, clothing, and shelter. Then one nurse decided to spend time with each child every day and hold them, hug them, and kiss them. These children started to put on weight, were more active, and started improving in their health. Love is so important to our health that we sometimes fail see the connection. God made us to have relationships...first with Him but also with one another.

Laugh and Play

I somewhat touched on this already, but this is a bit different. Laugh at their jokes, tell them jokes, run through the sprinkler with them, have a pillow fight with them, wash the car together and soak one another, jump in the pool and have a water fight with them, get the squirt guns out and squirt one another with water, tickle them, and spend quality time, at least fifteen minutes with each child, reading to them, play, and talking only to that one child. Special time with each child will help you draw closer to them.

Children are a gift of God and we must treat these precious ones, from newborns to teens and even into adulthood, with respect, love, and understanding, with the realization that they too were created in the image of God and He loves them more than we ever could.

Are you teaching the children in your life by saying or doing?

Deuteronomy 4:9 "Only take care, and keep your soul diligently, lest you forget the things that your eyes have seen, and lest they depart from your heart all the days of your life. Make them known to your children and your children's children."

What is Seen over What is Heard

I believe that we can talk till we're blue in the face but our actions will always drown out our words. Children can see right through hypocrisy a mile away. You just can't fool children. If our actions don't match our words, our words can be useless. Instead, let our actions do the talking for us. When our children hear us say things like "Tell them I'm not home" (after someone calls for you) or if we talk badly about someone behind their back after speaking to them in a nice way in front of them, children will see that our words mean nothing. They can't hear what we say if our actions are drowning out our words. They will do what you do, not necessarily what you say, so the question is, are we teaching our children by what we are saying more than by what we are doing? You surely know the answer to that.

Watch Your Actions

In the Old Testament, God frequently talked about what parents do more than what they say. Why? It's because our actions communicate more loudly than our words do. God tells parents to be careful and watch yourselves closely so that you do not forget the things your eyes have seen or let them fade from your heart as long as you live and make sure to teach them to your children and to their children after them (Duet 4:9). Notice that God said to be careful, watch our actions closely, don't' forget what our eyes have seen, don't let them fade from our memory and teach them to our children and even our grandchildren. This command is based upon what is seen more than what is said. God was concerned that our children learn to revere Him as long as they live and that means we must teach them to our children (Duet 4:10) but the best teacher is the visual one.

More is Caught than Taught

I believe it is true that more is caught than taught and the fact is that children may not hear what you are saying because your actions may be drowning out your words. It's hard to deceive children isn't it? You can teach them one thing but if we do something different, they can clearly see through our hypocrisy. If we teach our children one thing yet do just the opposite, we're really teaching them to do what we do rather than what we say. If they see you regularly reading your Bible, they'll see that you value the Word of God and the more you read the Bible to your children, and grandchildren for that matter, the more the Word of God will get into their minds and hearts and teaching our children is the best way to ensure that they might live a longer life (Duet 4:10).

I remember the story of a father who saw a tiny baby bird that had fell out of its nest. As his young son watched, the father took a ladder out of the garage and put on some latex gloves and lifted the tiny fledgling off the ground and placed it back into the nest. The boy asked his dad why he used the gloves. The boy's father said that if the mother had smelled the human scent then the mother would have rejected the young fledgling and the baby bird would have starved to death. By this father's tender, loving action, he taught the boy that we are to care for God's creatures because God loves His creation and His creatures too, although He loves us much more (Matt 10:31). The boy never forgot this and without a word, the boy's father taught the young child more than a hundred lectures ever could so again I would ask you and I ask myself this same question; are we teaching the children in our life by saying or by doing?

What Type Of Role Model Are You For Children In Your Life?

Deuteronomy 4:9 "Only take care, and keep your soul diligently, lest you forget the things that your eyes have seen, and lest they depart from your heart all the days of your life. Make them known to your children and your children's children."

Provoked to Anger

It is so easy for parents to provoke their children to anger and then have them grow discouraged (Col 3:21) but parents should bring up their children using discipline and instructing them in the ways of God but doing so out of love (Eph 6:4). If you are a grandparent, you are also told to teach them what you have learned from God as well (Duet 4:9). God the Father disciplines us since He corrects every one of His children (Heb 12:6) but He does it in love. We must model discipline in our own lives and in our children's lives for their own best interests, even when it goes against the grain of society. Just like a parent disciplines the children he or she loves, so too does God discipline us, His own children (Duet 8:5) and those who the Lord disciplines are actually blessed (Psalm 94:12). If we avoid disciplining children then it shows we really don't love them (Prov 13:24) so the way God looks at it is that love equals discipline and discipline equals love. I've talked to many prisoners who wished that their parents would have disciplined them more.

A Prayer for Your Child[ren]

Great God, You have given me my precious children and grandchildren as gift but they are only mine for a time...they are really Yours and I pray You keep them and protect them and bring them into a personal relationship with You and Your Great Son, Jesus Christ in whose name I pray.

3 Ways to Point Your Children to Christ

What are 3 ways that you can point your children to Jesus Christ as their Savior? What ways would you suggest?

Model Christ

I believe it is true...more is caught that taught, not that we shouldn't teach our children but from the child's perspective it's like this; "I can't hear what you are saying because what you are doing is drowning it out." Children can see through hypocrisy a mile away. When children see their parents loving one another and loving those who might even treat them disdainfully, they are taught, by example, how they are to treat others. Show them that our love for others is not dependent upon how others treat us because God loved us while we were still His enemies and living in sin (Rom 5:8, 10). When parents live out the Word of God out, it's impossible for children not to see it, but when they see their parents act one way at church and then live differently at home, they destroy their testimony for Christ.

Reading the Word

I don't know how many times my children would catch me reading my Bible. When they come to me, I would never say "Well, I'm too busy right now reading my Bible" but they see a regular pattern of Bible reading and it is my hope that they will see just how important regular, daily Bible reading is for me and hopefully, long after I am gone from this earth, they will remember that their dad was a consistent, regular Bible reader and that since I thought it was essential in my life, they too will see the importance of staying in the Word every day.

Praying Consistently

The old saying "The family that stays together, prays together" is absolutely true. Bill Bright once estimated that daily prayer, led by the parents, lessens the likelihood of divorce and when families stay together, the chances are so much greater that when their children marry, they'll stay together too. When families pray together, their children will be more likely to pray after they leave their homes and begin their own families. Prayer shows children the importance of keeping in daily contact with God and that they need God's guidance and direction in their lives and that they must depend upon God for everything in life. If God is aware of even the tiny sparrow that falls to the ground (Matt 10:29) we can know and we can show our children (and grandchildren) that God cares about every facet of their lives and that they must be relying upon Him for even the smallest details in their daily living experiences.

Parents can increase the chances of their children coming to saving faith in Jesus Christ by confessing their own faults, showing the love of God even to those who don't deserve it, by staying in the Word of God and showing the importance of the Bible in their lives and by staying in constant communication with the God that loves them even more than their parents do. Of course it doesn't guarantee they'll be saved but it does improve their chances of seeking Christ and His kingdom, even after you're long gone.

What Things Should Be Spoken of from the Bible?

5 Ways to Teach Your Children Respect

It is so important to teach children to respect; themselves, others, and society. What are 5 important ways that we can teach children respect?

Show them Respect

Just like adults, children are created in the image of God (Gen 1:26-27) and just as we treat adults, they should be treated with the same respect. If children grow up in an environment where they're being disrespected, why would we expect them to not treat others disrespectfully? I look at children as adults under construction but to God they have equal value and they are no less deserving of dignity and respect than any adult would be. This means that we don't berate them in public and humiliate them before others. If they need discipline, wait until you get home. I have heard parents actually swear at their children. This is nothing short of verbal abuse and there is no good excuse for this type of behavior…ever! Never yell, scream, or call your children names because this type of verbal damage goes deep and lasts for a very long time and may permanently damage the child. Words certainly do hurt and they can stay with them for a lifetime. When I taught in elementary school years ago as a substitute while finishing college, if I was ever asked a question by a child I never made them feel like their questions were stupid but "That's a very good question, I 'm glad you asked me that." I always used common courtesy like "yes ma'am," and "thank you sir" to the boys and girls so that they would see that I give them the same respect I give to the adults that they encounter in school. My oldest son heard me say that so much that he does the exact same thing when he greets people like "Yes sir" and "no thank you ma'am." Truly more is caught that taught.

Don't Label Them

Like a self-fulfilling prophecy, if you tell a child that they're stupid and won't ever amount to anything, they may just live that out in adulthood. Calling children names is labeling them and this hurts. I know what this feels like because it happened to me. We have a prison ministry and most of these men in prison had a father that mistreated them or abandoned them at an early age. This put so much pressure on the mother. The job of a single mother may be the most difficult job there is. She has to be the mother, the father, the nurse, the consultant, the bread winner, the maintenance person, and whatever else goes with being a parent and the list is quite long. If we tell children that they'll never amount to anything, guess what they shoot for? Treat them as you would want to be treated and name calling is labeling them. Teach them respect by respecting them.

Model Respect

This is where I say for sure that more is caught than it taught. You might not think so but your children are watching you. They are listening to you. They see how you treat others in the family or in public. They can hear how you talk to people but also how you talk about people, particularly when they aren't present. If you put down people behind their backs then your children might see that as a normal thing to do. If they see you treat others in public in a rude way, they'll know that this is the way that it's supposed to be. For good or bad, children imitate their parents and to a large extent, they grow up to be very much like them. If we are angry in rush hour traffic, if we are rude to the person at the fast-food counter, if we're impatient and grow angry if we have to wait for something or if we're quick tempered when things don't go our way, that's the way they'll possibly turn out. If we model respectful mannerisms and talk to people in person in the same way that we do when they're not there, then our children will learn what respect looks like and what it sounds like both in pubic and in private.

Love Their Father or Mother

When we show tender, loving care for our spouse, our children see that and they build their expectations and understandings around that about how to be a husband or wife when they grow up to be married, if indeed they do. Children might make faces when they see dad kiss mom or when mom hugs dad but deep down, it gives them a sense of security and stability. They need that grounded reassurance to know that even when times get tough, dad and mom work it out...they hang in there and stay together. When they don't yell, scream, shout, and call each other names, then they know that there are better ways to work out problems without having to lose control. If the parents do things for one another, serve one another, and esteem their spouse better than themselves, then they will know that each member of the household is supposed to contribute and they'll grow up with that expectation for marriage. Good parent's model treating each other with respect and this models respect to their children.

Acknowledge, Reward, and Reinforce

I used to tell children in the elementary school that "Aha! I caught you! I caught you doing something good!" They loved that. I think parents can model respect for children when they respect a job well done. There is nothing wrong with rewarding children when they meet or even exceed what was ask of them at home or for great marks or good behavior in school. It's not bribery when you do it after the fact. This reinforces the fact that you notice what they do and that they make you happy when they've done something well. I knew of a girl who got good grades in school but didn't really care about it because her parents wouldn't even take notice. In fact, if she got 5 A's and a B her parents wouldn't say, "Nice work, you worked hard and I appreciate your effort" but instead, they would say "Why'd you get a B in *that* class? What's wrong with you!?" When parents appreciate their children and show them respect for doing good then they are going to be more complimentary of others when they grow into adulthood but we need not overlook the fact that in their childhood, they'll be more positive and complimentary of others too.

The effect of showing and teaching children respect doesn't just come into fruition at adulthood. Showing them respect can positively affect them while they're still children so that they can enjoy their childhood and that's always a desired outcome of any parenting skills. Respect them and they will likely respect you and everyone else for that matter; in the least it'll give them a better chance that they'll respect others and you too.

How to Teach a Child to Memorize Bible Verses?

How can we help children commit to memory certain Bible verses? These same methods might also help adults do the very same thing.

In a Song

I believe one of the greatest ways to teach Scripture is using song. Songs have a way of imbedding themselves deep within the recesses of the mind. The notes tie in the lyrics or words into the melody and their memories retain it at a much higher rate than just rote memorization or reading and these biblically centered songs are still remembered and sung even into old age. Having them clap their hands to the music even further reinforces the memorization process. Even if they're not strictly Scripture, we can teach biblically centered lessons in songs and have the children memorize the stories in this way. It is a fun way to teach the children and what happens is that the adults teaching these scriptural songs and biblical stories end up memorizing them too and that surely a win-win.

Board Games

I don't know where my Bible board game went to but I used to use this in Sunday school when I taught 3rd/4th graders (combined). It was a board game where Moses was taking the Israelites out of Egypt toward the Promised Land and the children had to look at three different Bible verses to see which verse was right for where Israel was at the time. They learn to tie in the events of Genesis with the Scriptures associated with the migration of the nation of Israel after their exodus from Egypt. On the flip side, it was a board game about Joshua leading the nation into the Promised Land and just as in the other game on the flip side was, they had to select one of three Bible verses that matched where the Israelites were and that was the only way that they could advance on the game board. Each time they played it they became better at knowing which Bible verses were correct and after a while some didn't even need to look at the three choices given on Scripture card because they had memorized them.

Arts and Crafts

Children typically love arts and crafts and they can choose one of their favorite Bible verse and create a craft around it. It can be a Bible verse that can attach to a magnet and be placed on the refrigerator. It can be a small picture with a verse like "But as for me and my house, we will serve the LORD" (Joshua 24:15) and hung in the child's room where they can see it every day. The possibilities for biblical or scriptural arts and crafts are limited only by your and their imagination.

Dinner Table Scripture Reading

Take about thirty 3 by 5 index cards and write down, or better yet, have the children write down Bible verses and place them in a box that can be placed at the center of the dinner table. They can use different colored pencils to add some color to them. Before each meal have each child take out a Bible verse and have each one read theirs before the meal and prayer. These can be replaced every so often. This tradition works well for many families but is limited to the times when the family is actually gets together for a family meal, which seems to be a tradition that is slowly slipping away.

Make a Bible Verse Scrapbook

This is fun for the children too because they decide what Bible verses go in each page or section of a scrapbook. Make sure they have their own pictures and names on the inside liner or on the first page and put the dates that they were added. They can add pictures that they create and color or they can search old magazines or newspapers to clip out and paste, adding artwork that seems appropriate for the Bible verses they use. These little scrapbooks can become highly valued gems to cherish throughout the child's life that they can take with them into their adulthood and share with their own children.

Verse Around the Chairs

I couldn't come up with a good enough name for this one so I called it "Verse Around the Chairs" but have the children sit in a circle, on the floor or in chairs, and give each child a 3 by 5 index card with the same verse on it. Start randomly in one place and have each child read only one word at a time and immediately after one child reads one word of the Bible verse(s) have the child to their immediate right read the next and go around and around until the entire verse or verses are read. Start in the reverse order next time. Then challenge them to go as fast as they can...they'll love it. They will usually end up memorizing it fairly quick.

We are commanded by God to "take care, and keep your soul diligently, lest you forget the things that your eyes have seen, and lest they depart from your heart all the days of your life. Make them known to your children and your children's children" (Duet 4:9) "so that you, your children and their children after them may fear the LORD your God as long as you live by keeping all his decrees and commands that I give you, and so that you may enjoy long life" (Duet 6:2). Hey, maybe those are two Bible verses you can use to have your children to memorize.

4 Ugly Lies the World Is Trying To Teach Children

Here are 4 of the ugliest lies the world is teaching our children and grandchildren so you'll know what you're up against as a parent, foster parent, or grandparent.

Molecules to Man

The theory of evolution reduces children into thinking that they're only an accident of nature, a random occurrence of blind chance with no intelligent designer and that they live on a lucky planet found in what is called "the Goldilocks Zone" of our solar system where the chance for life was fortunately increased because of where the earth is placed. The world teaches children they're evolved from animals and then they're surprised when they sometimes act like one. This lie teaches children that they have no true purpose, they have no future beyond the grave, and that it is a dog-eat-dog world and survival of the fittest is the name of the game.

It's Okay to Lie

I took an ethics class in college and it angered me that some of the students thought that it's okay to lie. Strangely, the professor saw no problem with this. It is not okay to lie? Sorry. When the professor said it was okay to lie, he actually committed a lie right there. The Bible says that all liars will have their part in the lake of fire (Rev 21:8) so sorry professor, you are wrong. How said to tell students it's okay to lie. Would the professor really want the students to lie to him about why they missed an assignment, or why they missed class, or make an excuse for a false "death in the family" lie just so that they could get out of class?

The Bible is not True

This one is interesting. I had a young man try to refute the Bible's authenticity by saying that it was written by man. He said that his biology, history, and science textbooks showed him what is really true. I asked him "Who wrote these books? Weren't they also written by men?" He acknowledge my point but then he said "The Bible is full of errors" so I asked him to show me where they were. He waffled and then I asked him, "Do you use the same science textbook you used 10 years ago?" He said, no. Then I asked him why not and he said, they've been revised and updated. Why? Because they've found some errors and new discoveries had to replace the mistakes in the old science books. He saw my point. Textbooks necessarily have to be revised every few years because they find mistakes and new information has to be added. Not so with the Bible. It stands the test of time, unlike books written by the so-called "educated" of the world.

Man is Basically Good

Really?! Doesn't the Bible say that "All have turned aside; together they have become worthless; no one does good, not even one" (Rom 3:12) and "The heart is deceitful above all things, and desperately sick" (Jer 17:9) and Jesus said that "No one is good except God alone" (Mark 10:18). Nope, we've all fallen short...way short...of the glory of God (Rom 3:23). God alone is good and mankind in our fallen nature is not but we can be forgiven by a good God and made the very righteousness of God by Jesus' atoning payment and death

(2 Cor 5:21).

Our children and grandchildren will hear many lies in the world, even in our schools, so parents must rely on God alone for truth and it is found in His Word because only God cannot lie (Num 23:19; Titus 1:2) so you can trust what you read in His Word. Of that you can be 100% sure.

5 Self Examination Questions for the Christian Dad

Here are 5 self-examination questions for the Christian dad to ask himself. What ones would you include?

What is your Prayer Quotient?

I sometimes ask myself: "What is the amount of time that I spend praying for my children?" This is a very convicting question because I know I fall way short of how much time I should be spending in prayer. I'm throwing myself under the bus on this one...I need to be praying daily and consistently for my children/grandchildren.

How Much Time do you Listen?

Again, I plead guilty to this...do I spend enough time just listen to my children? Do I try to not interrupt them when they are speaking? I need to not just hear what they are saying but to listen to what they are trying to tell me.

How Much Do I Compliment Them?

I grew up never hearing any praise or compliments, only complaints and harsh words so I wanted to break that cycle. I try to be complimenting my children or grandchildren frequently and be very specific like on their report card, the way the cleaned their room, or whatever and not just flatter them...doing it in all sincerity. They can spot phony praise a mile away.

Do I put God First?

I think children actually love it when dads put God first. Despite what you may think, if dads will put God first that means that they'll be a better dad. If God is that "third cord" in the home, then the children will be the beneficiaries in the short term and in the long run. That's because two Christian parents are good but when God is that "threefold cord" the home "is not quickly broken" (Eccl 4:12).

Do I Love Their Mother?

I know this might not seem to fit but even if your children cover their eyes and say "gross" when you kiss and hug their mother, inwardly that makes them feel secure. They believe that if you love their mother in a profound and meaningful way, then they'll feel like the home has a more sure foundation. When all other homes might be breaking apart at the seams, loving their mother seems like the glue that holds it securely in place. Loving their mother is essentially loving them. Am I showing genuine affection toward their mother? Am I complimentary and thankful to her in words and in action?

3 prayers that you can pray over your child today

That God Will Call Them

I love the idea of praying for children to come to saving faith in Jesus Christ. We know that salvation is fully a work of God (Eph 2:8-9) but we also know that God's will is that all should come to repentance and faith in Christ (1 Tim, 2:4) so when you pray for your children to be saved we know that this is God's will and so pray for them in this way; Oh righteous Father, please send Your Spirit to convict my children of their sin and to see their need for You and the Son of God as their Savior. We know that this is Your will and I so desire, as You do as well, that they might be saved and put their trust in Christ and this will bring You glory. In Jesus Righteous Name I pray, amen.

That Prodigals Will Repent and be Saved

There may be nothing more heartbreaking than to have children grow up in the knowledge of the Lord and thinking that they were saved only to leave home and abandon their faith. Is there anything more painful than knowing that your children are living in a sinful lifestyle and that they are far from the Lord? Pray for these prodigals and never give up. I heard of one mother who prayed for 35 years and her son finally repented and put his trust in Christ so pray like this; Please help me Lord to have the faith to keep on praying and never give up, even though he/she is not living in obedience to You right now. Please forgive me where I fell short in raising my prodigal when he/she was young. Please help me to persevere and continue to pray in the hopes that they might return to You and once more live a life that is pleasing to You. In Jesus' Holy Name, amen.

That God Will Keep them from Temptations and Sin

We know that there are wicked spirits in high places and that the Enemy would love nothing more than to bring down your children and cause them to stumble into serious sin. Christian parents, you must realize that your children have a bulls eye on them and Satan and his minions would love nothing more than to have them fall into his traps. We know that God loves our children more than we do so pray like this; Father, You love our child[ren] more than we do so please help them to avoid things, places, or people that might cause them to be tempted and fall into sin. I beg You to not allow them to be in situations where they might cave into peer pressure and convict them with Your Spirit to avoid sinning and have Your ways brought to mind when they consider doing something sinful. I pray these things in the Mighty Name of Jesus Christ, amen.

Conclusion

Don't ever stop praying for your children. God never gives up on us and He never gives up on our children either. Pray that, if they haven't yet been saved, that they might believe in Jesus Christ, that if they are prodigals, that they will repent and return again to the Lord, and to keep them away from tempting situations where they might sin and convict them by His Spirit to stop before they do.

Parents, grandparents, foster parents, and all caregivers, we only get one shot with these children so pray daily, ask counsel in His Word, the Bible, and be honest with children. Admit your mistakes and that you're not perfect. They already know it anyway. Transparency is so important to children. I believe the eight more important words that we can say to our children in our life time are these; "I love you," "I'm sorry," and "Please forgive me."

Teaching Children the Gospel, 3rd Volume. Copyright © 2015 by Jack Wellman
ISBN 1449996388   EAN-13 9781449996383
All rights reserved. No part of this book may be reproduced or transmitted in any form or by any means without written permission from the author. To contact the author, please email him at: jackwellman@hotmail.com
Printed in USA.

Other books from this author include *Do Babies Go to Heaven, Blind Chance or Intelligent Design: Empirical Methodologies and the Bible,* and *The Great Omission; Reaching the Lost for the Great Commission*

- Evolution is a theory, not a scientific law.
- Evolution can not be validated
  - can not be proven through Scientific methods
  - can it be observed in a lab
  - can it be repeated
  - is it predictable

- Theory to Law
  - observed
  - repeated
  - not predictable

- Theory based on assumptions.
- What is missing... the gaps of transitional fossils, that establish one species evolving into another, new specie
- When a missing link is found? Where is the chain.